D0914543

The Curti Lectures

The University of Wisconsin–Madison
September 1982

To honor the distinguished historian Merle Curti,
lectures in social and intellectual history
were inaugurated in 1976 under the sponsorship of the
University of Wisconsin Foundation and the
Department of History of the University of Wisconsin-Madison.

Published by the University of Wisconsin Press

Christopher Hill, *Some Intellectual Consequences of the English Revolution* (1980)

Carlo M. Cipolla, *Fighting the Plague in Seventeenth-Century Italy* (1981)

James Willard Hurst, *Law and Markets in United States History: Different Modes of Bargaining among Interests* (1982)

The End of Prussia

Gordon A. Craig

THE UNIVERSITY OF WISCONSIN PRESS

Published 1984

The University of Wisconsin Press
114 North Murray Street
Madison, Wisconsin 53715

The University of Wisconsin Press, Ltd.
1 Gower Street
London WC1E 6HA, England

First printing

Printed in the United States of America

For LC CIP information see the colophon

ISBN 0-299-09730-7

Contents

The End
of Prussia

Introduction

Periodization has always fascinated historians, and there are those among us who are never happier than when they are arguing about the proper dates for the beginnings and ends of things.[1] When I was a graduate student, it seemed to me that, whenever I thought I was beginning to get it all straightened out, someone in authority decided that things weren't as simple as that; so that if I took the word of Burckhardt and wrote into my copybook that the Renaissance began in Italy in the *quattrocento,* I would almost immediately come upon an article stating that it happened in some other country, and in the twelfth century. Indeed, for a time it seemed to me that there was a kind of cottage industry in our discipline busily turning out new beginnings for the Renaissance.

I was reminded of this three years ago when I became a member of the board of consultants to the planning staff for the Prussian Exhibition in Berlin in 1981, for much of the board's time in the early stages was given over to protracted and heated debate over when Prussian history began and when it ended, eminently practical issues for the planning staff, since the assignment of exhibition rooms depended upon how they were settled. More recently, in one of the most interesting of the books that comprised the so-called Prussian Wave of 1980–81,[1] Rudolf von Thadden discusses this question of dating at some length and shows how perplexing it is. One can make a good case, he points out, for placing the beginning of Prussia in the

---

1. Rudolf von Thadden, *Fragen an Preussen: Zur Geschichte eines aufgehobenen Staates* (Munich, 1981).

High Middle Ages, with the establishment of the so-called Or-densland of the Teutonic Knights, for, after all, the modern kingdom of Prussia owed both its name and its claim to kingly rank to that early colonization. But for every historian to take that position there is another at variance with him. The year 1415, when rule over the Mark Brandenburg passed to the House of Hohenzollern, and with it one of the seven electorates of the Holy Roman Empire, has its strong advocates. Frederick the Great, a not inconsiderable historian in his leisure hours, placed the date much later, writing in his *Mémoires pour servir à l'histoire de la maison de Brandebourg* (1751): "The history of Brandenburg begins to be interesting only with [Kurfürst] Jo-hann Sigismund [at the beginning of the seventeenth century], through his acquisition of Prussia but also of the succession to Cleves, to which he acquired legal title by marriage. Only from that point on did the area begin to acquire a fullness and af-forded even me the means for suitable expansion." Heinrich von Treitschke, the most Prussian of nineteenth-century historians, insisted that Prussian history really began with the Thirty Years War and the raising of the first truly native army by the Great Elector Frederick William. The debate shows no sign of flag-ging. *Tot gestarum scriptores quot sententiae.*

The question of Prussia's end is, in Thadden's opinion, even more vexing. Of the four dates most usually suggested — 1871, 1919, 1932, and 1947 — the first three seem to be premature and the fourth belated. To argue, as some historians have, that Prussia came to an end with the proclamation of the empire at Versailles is to overlook the vigor with which it asserted its autonomy within the new Reich and the constitutional and struc-tural problems that resulted from that circumstance. To hold with others that Prussia died when the Hohenzollerns were ex-pelled and the old Prussian army dissolved is to close one's eyes to the strength of Prussian monarchism and militarism during the Weimar Republic. Even the so-called *Preussenschlag* of July

1932, when Reich Chancellor Franz von Papen deprived Prussia's last legitimate government of its functions and submitted the land to the rule of Reich commissioners, could hardly be considered as a death blow, since in the subsequent period both Adolf Hitler and those who sought to kill him in 1944 invoked the spirit of Potsdam to justify their actions.

Yet, if these dates won't do, nor will that of 25 February 1947, when Lieutenant Generals Lucius D. Clay, Sir Brian Robinson, and Joseph-Pierre Koenig and Marshal Vassily Sokolovsky, acting in the name of the Allied Control Council in Berlin, signed what was called Law No. 46. Justifying their action with the argument that "the Prussian state [had] from early days . . . been the bearer of militarism and reaction in Germany," and stating that the new law was in harmony with "the interests of preservation of peace and security of peoples and with the desire to assure further reconstruction of the political life of Germany on a democratic basis," the four generals decreed that "the Prussian state with its central government and all its agencies is abolished."[2] The only trouble was, as they themselves admitted rather lamely, that Prussia had already ceased to exist in any real geographic or demographic sense, for its population was dispersed, its eastern provinces had been absorbed by the Russians and the Poles, and its western ones divided and assigned to new political jurisdictions, so that in the consciousness of most Germans it was already part of a dead past, and the decree a belated act that appeared to limp in the wake of history.

With reference to the end of Prussia, then, Thadden concluded that none of the proposed dates satisfied the historian's striving for unambiguousness, and that we were left with the problem that we had started with. "We know," he wrote, "that Prussia is dead and can be revived only at the cost of violating

2. Herbert Michaelis and Ernst Schraepeler, eds., *Ursachen und Folgen vom deutschen Zusammenbruch 1918 und 1945,* vol. XXIII (Berlin, n.d.), p. 372.

the corpse. But we are not in a position to . . . terminate its history in a satisfactory manner."[3]

But surely the pragmatism that is characteristic of western historiography is not incapable of relieving this perhaps needlessly convoluted problem. Can we not avoid the question of dating entirely by regarding the end of Prussia not as an event but as a process? It has always seemed to me that the final phase of Prussian history was announced on that dark October afternoon in 1806 when Prince Louis Ferdinand, the *beau sabreur* of the Prussian army, was killed at Saalfeld in a firefight with Murat's light cavalry, an event that spread panic and confusion in the hastily mobilized forces that stood at Weimar and opened the way for their shattering defeat at Jena and Auerstedt a few days later. That repulse, which Queen Luise sought to explain with the rueful words, "We fell asleep on the laurels of Frederick the Great," was catastrophic, and although Prussia in time recovered from it in a physical sense, an irreparable blow had been inflicted on the reputation that it had enjoyed under Frederick as the land of unlimited possibilities, the most energetic, modern, and progressive state in Europe. From that loss there proved to be no recovery, even though, in the course of the century and a quarter that followed, there were periodically opportunities which, if seized, might have allowed Prussia to regain its old spiritual momentum and to become what it had shown signs of becoming at the end of the eighteenth century. But, as we shall see, these chances were let slip, or the wrong choices were made, and the country moved, with deliberate speed and majestic instancy, toward the cold and cheerless twilight that awaited it.

There are many ways in which we might observe this fateful process or, if you will, this slow death. I have chosen in these lectures to do so through the eyes and the activities of a few

3. *Fragen*, pp. 23–24.

individuals at four distinct periods in late Prussian history, starting with Freiherr Karl Friedrich vom Stein and F. A. L. von der Marwitz in the so-called Period of Reform after 1807, and then, in subsequent lectures, going on to consider Bettina von Arnim and the young Bismarck in the 1840s; the novelist Theodor Fontane and Emperor William II after Prussia had unified Germany; and finally, in the Weimar period, the socialist minister president of Prussia Otto Braun, and the Rhineland politician Konrad Adenauer.

CHAPTER 1

The Failure of Reform:
Stein and Marwitz

I

To choose Stein for special attention should cause no great surprise. As Barbara Vogel has pointed out recently, in German historiography he has always enjoyed a respect that is inversely proportional to the modesty of his tangible accomplishments as a reformer, and in contemporary Germany he is the only historical figure upon whose stature both bourgeois and Marxist historians seem to agree. In Gebhardt, the leading West German historical handbook, he is described as "in fact the best statesman at Germany's disposal in his time"; in the East German equivalent, *Deutsche Geschichte in drei Bänden,* he appears as "the most significant German statesman in the first half of the nineteenth century," and in the recent East German television series "Scharnhorst" he was accorded a veneration bordering upon glorification. One need not, then, apologize for his inclusion here, but why should his name be paired with that of Marwitz, a country squire and sometime soldier who has attracted no attention outside of his own country and relatively little within, except for some forgotten monographs, a tendentious Nazi biography, and a fictional portrait in Fontane's first novel?

It is, in fact, a coupling that is not difficult to justify. Among the leading figures of the generation that experienced the collapse of Prussia in 1806, Marwitz came closer to resembling

Stein in the depth and unconditionality of his moral and political convictions than anyone else except perhaps Scharnhorst. In the fight to free Prussia from the yoke of Napoleon in the subsequent period, he was Stein's natural ally, for if Stein's was the voice that aroused what Meinecke called the heroic storm of the liberation, Marwitz was an influential leader of the country nobility who flocked to the colors when their king's cause was in danger and carried the brunt of the battle. But in this collaboration there was a more basic and irremediable antagonism, for the Prussia that Marwitz wished to save was not the one that Stein wanted to survive; and from this fundamental disagreement stemmed not only the essential failure of the reform movement of the years 1807–13 but a more basic dichotomy that was to dominate Prussian politics for the next century and a quarter. Marwitz's role in Prussian history was far from trivial. It has been said of him that he created the first effective political opposition in the country. It became, as it happened, an opposition to every progressive tendency that Stein had sought to encourage.

Conflict between the two was perhaps rooted in the nature and difference of their Prussianism. Stein, of course, was by birth and background not a Prussian at all but a West German whose family seat had stood since the year 1235 in the town of Nassau and whose estates were scattered along the Rhine and the Lahn. He was, moreover, an imperial knight (*Reichsritter*), with all the privileges that that implied—the protection of the imperial law and the *Reichsgerichte* in disputes with his more powerful princely neighbors, an intimate and direct relationship with the emperor himself if he cared to enter into his service, and a proud sense of being at the same time independent and part of a long religiopolitical tradition. Treitschke's description of Stein, although in the rhetoric of an age that admired purple passages, shrewdly suggests that his appearance and his characteristic style were not uninfluenced by his pride in what he was:

the thickset figure with the wide neck, the strong shoulders that seemed formed for armor, deep sparkling brown eyes under the mighty housing of the brow, an owl's nose over the small expressive lips, every movement of the big hands rapid, angular, peremptory, a character as if from out of the high-minded sixteenth century that involuntarily reminded one of Dürer's portrait of Ritter Franz von Sickingen—so gifted and so simple, so bold among men, so humble before God—the whole man a wonderful combination of natural strength and cultivation [*Bildung*], of liberality of mind and justice, of glowing passion and reasoned calculation.[1]

Yet, when this *Reichsfreiherr* was a young man and had to choose a career, he did not do the obvious thing and turn to Vienna, where a predictably honorable and lucrative one awaited him in the imperial service. Instead, in 1780, he petitioned for admission to the civil service of the king of Prussia, partly because of special opportunities to indulge a passion for mining studies, but certainly also—as we know from his writings—because of his admiration of Frederick the Great and of the liberality of the Prussian system, which showed no prejudice against energetic outsiders and offered them responsibility and advancement. And his faith was justified, for in the next twenty-four years he moved rapidly upward in the bureaucratic hierarchy, from supervisor of the Westphalian mining department, to director of the chamber in Cleves, and finally to the post of *Oberpräsident,* the highest administrative post in Prussia's western province. Along the way he acquired a reputation for technical mastery of economic and financial matters, imagination and initiative as an administrator, and the authority of the natural leader, and it did not cause any surprise when Frederick William III, faced with mounting fiscal difficulties, summoned him in 1804 to come to Berlin and assume the duties of minister

1. Heinrich von Treitschke, *Deutsche Geschichte im neunzehnten Jahrhundert,* 5 vols. (Leipzig, 1879–99), I, 275.

of taxes and tolls and director of the department of factories and commerce. Stein never found the Prussian capital congenial but accepted, writing to the royal counsellor Karl Friedrich Beyme, "When one is inwardly convinced that Germany's improvement and culture are tied firmly and irreparably to the fortunes of the Prussian monarchy, then one cannot for a moment waver between duty and personal caprice"[2] — words that indicated that his Prussian sentiment was as strong as it had been in his youth but was now informed by his faith in what Prussia could do, not for him, but for Germany. In this sense, during his long years in the civil service, Stein had not succeeded in overcoming his imperial heritage.

Marwitz suffered from none of this ambivalence, for his Prussianism was unalloyed. There had been Marwitzes in Pomerania as early as the thirteenth century; Ludwig von der Marwitz's forebears had served the Teutonic Order in the Neumark in the fifteenth century; and his own estate at Friedersdorf had been in the family since the early seventeenth century. As a landowner, he was proud of being a member of the first estate of the realm and conscious of the duties this imposed on him: to the soil (he was an industrious and progressive farmer, whose experiments attracted visitors from Weimar and Schleswig-Holstein and interested Albrecht Thaer's Agricultural Society), and to his king in terms of military service. There had always been Marwitzes in the army. Seven of them (he was to be the eighth) had attained general's rank, a record exceeded only by the Kleists, the Schwerins, the Goltzes, the Borcks, and the Bredows. In the wars of Frederick the Great, twelve Marwitzes were engaged, of whom six fell in the Seven Years War and four won the order *Pour le mérite*. In 1790, at the age of thirteen, still too young to manage heavy cavalry horses, Ludwig

2. *Freiherr vom Stein in Selbstzeugnissen und Bilddokumenten*, ed. Georg Holmsten (Reinbek, 1975), p. 33.

von der Marwitz took a commission in the Regiment Gens-darmes and served intermittently, and always in time of war, until 1827. His Prussianism, in short, was simpler than Stein's, circumscribed by the traditions and values of his estate, and un-affected by the bureaucratic liberalism that had attracted Stein to Prussia or by any thoughts of a Prussian mission in Germany. But there was no apparent reason why their differing views of Prussia should have brought them into conflict. It was Napo-leon Bonaparte who caused that to happen.

II

When Stein came to Berlin as finance minister, he was appalled at what he found. While the rest of Europe had been at war, Prussia had remained neutral since the Peace of Basel in 1795, but the results had been debilitating and, to Stein's moral sense, reprehensible. The upper classes, not excluding the court, seemed intent only upon frivolous amusement and the pursuit of lux-ury, and the signs of moral laxity seemed to justify the claim of the editor of the *Preussische Staatsanzeiger* that "one could call Berlin the great Babylon." In this atmosphere, the govern-ment seemed bereft of both vigor and efficiency. The general directory, which had been founded by Frederick William I, had ballooned into dozens of competing administrations and minis-tries with no clear authority and no ready access to anyone who could supply it. Without the ability or the energy of his great predecessors, Frederick William III insisted upon following their example and retaining the right of final decision on policy mat-ters. In practice, this meant that his cabinet secretaries—Beyme for internal affairs, Lombard for foreign affairs, Köckritz for mili-tary affairs—told him how he should decide, often doing so on the basis of information supplied, not by responsible ministers, but by personal friends, interested parties, or hangers-on at court.

This was not a system that would be tolerable to the impetuous Rhinelander. Friedrich Meinecke once wrote that Stein brought the *furor teutonicus* into German politics, and one is inclined to agree when one reads of his stormy passages through the general directory, his blistering complaints to the cabinet secretaries about delays in responding to his memoranda, his furious campaign against the practice of advancing state loans to aristocratic confidence men without demanding security, his violent attacks upon peculation. "Go! Don't besmirch my eyes!" he shouted to one dishonest tax collector. "God has given the king the right of pardon, but no king can make an honorable man out of a scoundrel! Out! Down those stairs! Or I'll show you how!"[3] This was unheard-of behavior, but it brought results: Stein reformed customs regulations, abolished restrictive guild and manufacturing privileges, established a bureau of economic statistics, and drafted a schedule of new taxes against the crisis that he felt was impending.

It was inevitable that his influence would not be restricted to finances. As early as the autumn of 1805, he wrote to the king predicting that Napoleon's excessive ambition would sooner or later force Prussia to go to war. This had no effect upon Frederick William III, whose statecraft was, Stein once said, "wavering, hesitant, and intent solely upon the maintenance of peace from moment to moment."[4] Like his ancestor Georg Friedrich at the beginning of the Thirty Years War, he clung desperately to neutrality; but under France's remorseless pressure he showed himself willing in the end, for the sake of peace, not only to accept a French alliance but also to close his North Sea ports to British shipping.

These capitulations, which were ruinous economically and promised to invite war with Britain and Russia, drove Stein into

3. Ibid., p. 39.
4. Freiherr vom Stein, *Denkwürdigkeiten und Briefe,* ed. L. Lorenz (Berlin, 1919), p. 308.

an open offensive against the king's policy and advisors. His campaign opened with a memorandum of April 1806 which included Stein's first proposal for a basic reform of the central government. This memorandum was so violent in its language (the foreign minister, Haugwitz, was described as "a man without rectitude, a worn-out voluptuary carousing in sensual pleasures," and Köckritz, the military adviser, as "limited and uneducated, . . . of common character and manner of thought")[5] that Stein's friends persuaded him not to send it to the king but to rely on a more indirect approach. His views were, however, well known and, because of the vigor with which he expressed them, he came to be considered as the leader of those officials, courtiers, soldiers, and intellectuals who wanted to change the direction of Prussian policy before it was too late. The most vocal of these included Prince Louis Ferdinand, a handsome man with many talents and the hero of the junior officers, his brother-in-law Prince Radziwill, General Prince von Hohenlohe, the historian Johannes von Müller, the scholars Ancillon and Alexander von Humboldt, and two of the king's brothers. Not unnaturally, the king regarded this combination as a *fronde* and, when he received another memorandum from them in August, drafted by Müller but expressing Stein's ideas, he responded with petulance and threats of disciplinary action against the soldiers.

While this was going on, Marwitz was tending his crops at Friedersdorf. If he knew of the oppositional activity, he probably disapproved of it, not because he was happy with the course of Prussian policy, for he was not, but rather because of some of the *fronde*'s members. Stein he did not know, but he disapproved of Prince Louis Ferdinand's reputation for libertinism

5. *Die Reorganisation des preussischen Staates unter Stein und Hardenberg,* ed. G. Winter (Berlin, 1931), Part I, Volume I, No. 5; Gerhard Ritter, *Stein: Eine politische Biographie* (new ed., Stuttgart, 1958), p. 152.

and his predilection for friends among the Berlin *haute volée* who frequented Rahel Levin's salon, and he thoroughly distrusted Johannes von Müller, the self-appointed secretary of the opposition. He called Müller "an ugly *Kerlchen* with a paunch and little legs and a fat face always glowing from eating and drinking,"[6] and his suspicions of his motives proved to be justified when Müller, shortly after Jena, went over to Napoleon and accepted office under him. Marwitz preferred his rural cares to intercourse with such people. He was not, however, allowed to enjoy them for much longer. By the fall of 1806, the futility of the king's policy was painfully apparent; in September, Marwitz received an urgent message from Prince Hohenlohe, ordering him to join his command; and on 14 October he was on the stricken field of Jena when the French, under Napoleon's personal command, cut Hohenlohe's corps to pieces. In that day's fighting, Marwitz had a horse shot from under him and his hat riddled with bullets, and he repeatedly led wavering troops back into the fight. This did no good. Hohenlohe was able to detach twelve thousand men from the battle and to make his way to Prenzlau, but he was a broken man and, instead of seeking to make a junction with other units, he listened to the advice of his defeatist chief of staff, Massenbach, and laid down his arms.

Ironically, this shameful defeat, the consequences of which were in the end to turn Stein and Marwitz into enemies, made them for a brief period collaborators in a lost cause. Humiliated by Hohenlohe's capitulation, Marwitz resolved to join the king and place his sword at his disposal and, by heroic efforts, did just that. Escaping from Prenzlau, he managed to join Blücher's corps and accompany it as far as Strelitz. From here, at the end of November, by avoiding main routes, he slipped into neutral

6. See Theodor Fontane, *Sämtliche Werke,* Nymphenburg edition, ed. Edgar Gross, 24 vols. (Munich, 1959–75), X, 222.

Swedish territory and, with a forged pass, traveled by sea from Stralsund to Ysted, and then in an eight-day voyage by small boat from Malmö to Copenhagen, and thence by British warship to Danzig, where he hired post horses and completed the journey to Königsberg, reporting to the king on 17 December. Despite the rigors of his long journey, he was full of energy and anxious to play his part in a joint Russo-Prussian offensive that would wipe out the memory of Jena and Prenzlau. But he soon discovered that Frederick William was unwilling to discuss the causes of the collapse or even hear about the personal failure of Hohenlohe and Massenbach at Prenzlau; and, in the royal entourage, he found only one person whose combative instinct matched his own, and that was Stein.

To the news of 14 October, Stein had reacted with his customary vigor. He immediately ordered all of the reserves of gold in the finance ministry's various accounts to be packed and shipped to Königsberg via Stettin, an action that kept the court solvent during the critical months that followed; and then, although he was suffering painfully from gout, he set on the way himself. He was thus able to play a decisive role in persuading the king at Osterode not to agree to an armistice with Napoleon, arguing that, if he did so, the Corsican would use Prussian territory to make a settlement with Britain and Russia. He urged a vigorous persecution of the war and the beginning of basic reform in the structure of the state so as to support it.

But the king's mind still ran toward peace, and he wanted Stein to assume the post of foreign minister in order to pursue it. Stein's refusal to consider this request, on the grounds that this was no time for him to learn a new job and that the reform of the cabinet system and the introduction of ministerial responsibility should receive first priority, touched off a royal explosion, the famous letter in which Frederick William wrote that Stein's recalcitrance had convinced him that:

unfortunately I was not wrong in my first judgment of you and that you are a refractory, insolent, obstinate and disobedient official. . . . I have given you my opinion in good German, and I must add that, if you are not willing to change your disrespectful and improper behavior, the state can place no great reliance upon your further service.[7]

On receipt of this letter, Stein immediately submitted his resignation. It was 4 January 1807, barely three weeks after Marwitz arrived in Königsberg, and he wrote in his diary:

The last support of the state on the civilian side, Minister Stein, receives his dismissal. I rode away with heavy heart. I saw no salvation for the state and no prospect for me to be useful to it.[8]

Indeed, what energy there was in royal headquarters seemed to disappear with Stein's departure. Marwitz himself went to Memel and raised a free corps for the hoped-for Russo-Prussian offensive, but the allies could never agree on a strategic plan, and as usual Napoleon anticipated them. In July, it was all over; a dismembered Prussia lay at the emperor's feet; and Marwitz was making his way back to his devastated and plundered estate.

III

It was at this low point in the country's fortunes that Stein made his great appeal for national regeneration. In the Nassau Memorandum of June 1807—which Theodor Heuss once called a document unique in German history for its combination of concreteness and moral eloquence—he declared that the crisis made it necessary "to strengthen the government through the knowledge and the esteem of all the educated classes, to bind

---

7. Stein, *Briefe und amtliche Schriften,* ed. W. Hubatsch, 10 vols. (Stuttgart, 1957–74), II, 329 f.; Ritter, *Stein,* p. 178.
8. Walther Kayser, *Marwitz* (Hamburg, 1936), p. 131.

them all to the state through conviction, participation, and collaboration in the national business, to give the energies of the nation free play, and to focus them on subjects of the common welfare." The goal should now be "the awakening of community spirit and civic conscience, the utilization of the sleeping and misdirected forces and the dispersed and unused skills, harmony between the spirit of the nation and its desires and needs and those of the agencies of the state, and the reawakening of a feeling for fatherland, independence, and national honor." This would require attention to the legitimate needs of the masses, for "if the nation is to be raised in dignity, its depressed parts must be given freedom, independence, and property and the protection of the laws, [and] the improvement and building of educational institutions, particularly rural schools, must go forward, so that a great mass of basic skills spreads through the nation."9

These general principles were given concrete form when, in October 1807, the king was persuaded to swallow his pride and his reservations concerning the strong-willed minister and to place the direction of all internal affairs in his hands. Stein immediately embarked on the program that was to bring the abolition of hereditary serfdom in the month of his appointment, the institution of local government in the cities in the following year, some important educational innovations, and a basic reform of the structure and disciplinary codes of the army and of the social composition of its officer corps—and which he hoped would be crowned by a thoroughgoing reform of the central government and the establishment of some form of national representation. Had this program been implemented in the spirit of its author, German history might have taken a different course, Prussia's role in 1848 and in the unification of Germany been different, and the attainment of democracy been

9. *Briefe und amtliche Schriften,* II, 397.

speedier and more secure. But, as we know, those reforms that were put into effect were, with the exception of the city ordinance, limited in their original application and sooner or later amended in crippling or nugatory ways, and the idea of a constitution guaranteeing a representative parliament for the whole realm remained an idle dream until the mid-century. Why, we should ask, was this failure so complete?

One reason was certainly that Stein's personal direction of affairs was so short, and for this he was himself in part responsible. He was always an impetuous and headstrong man and, under the influence of great emotion, incautious. In the fall of 1808, Napoleon's difficulties in Spain filled Stein's mind with visions of popular insurrections throughout the length and breadth of Germany that would be the occasion of Prussia's liberation. On 15 August, he wrote to a confidant of the king, Prince Wittgenstein, who was visiting Holstein, about his hopes, speaking of the necessity of establishing secret ties with patriotic elements in other German states, urging Wittgenstein to do his best to spread the news concerning Spain, and expressing confidence that, if a war broke out in Austria, as seemed likely, "it would decide Europe's fate and our own."[10] This letter was intercepted by French military police and printed in full in *Le Moniteur,* and Stein's position became untenable. Indeed, in an action that was extraordinary for a head of state, Napoleon issued an army order in Spain that declared Stein to be an enemy of France and, in a letter to the French foreign minister, ordered that Stein's estates were to be sequestrated and that, if he were seized by French troops, he was to be shot. Stein was forced to go into exile, and the strongest impulse behind the reform movement disappeared.

The reforms failed, in the second place, because Stein's successor, Hardenberg, approached them with a different spirit and

10. Ibid., II, 817.

set of priorities. As Gerhard Ritter points out, Hardenberg was more interested in developing a bureaucratically centralized chancellorship on the French model than in encouraging the middle-class participation in government that Stein regarded as essential. Under Hardenberg's direction, Stein's liberalism was replaced by an *étatisme* that was doubtless more efficient than the old cabinet system but was far from being either representative or national. In addition, Hardenberg was, by training and temperament, a diplomat, which allowed him to condone compromises that Stein would have rejected with indignation, and made him disinclined to have Prussia appear to be more progressive than its allies in the conservative post-Napoleonic world. Stein himself blamed Hardenberg for not pushing the reforms, attributing his lack of energy to inadequate knowledge of internal affairs, poor judgment in appointments, and — characteristic of Stein's stern morality — "his intimate intercourse with worthless women."[11]

But the most important reason for the failure of the reforms was that the old Prussia, the Prussia of clearly differentiated *Stände* (estates) and dominated by crown and landed nobility and army, was stronger and more resilient than Stein, for one, had imagined, and its recovery stifled the reforming tendency. And in this process Ludwig von der Marwitz played a leading role.

Marwitz's admiration of Stein did not long survive that minister's recall to office. If he was at first inclined to agree with the Rhenish *Freiherr* that the basic cause of the collapse of 1806 was moral and spiritual in nature, he soon became convinced that the minister's reforms were not likely to correct that condition. His objections were spelled out after Stein's second dismissal in a detailed critique of Stein's farewell message to his supporters. In this document, sometimes called Stein's "testa-

11. Stein, *Denkwürdigkeiten*, p. 324.

ment," which was drafted by his associate Theodor von Schön, Stein pointed out that the goal of his ministry had been to "put an end to the disharmony that had existed among the people, to destroy the conflict between the separate estates of the realm, which makes us unhappy, to provide by law the possibility that every individual among the people can give free moral expression to his powers, and thus to oblige the people to love king and fatherland in such a way that they will gladly sacrifice their property and blood for him."[12] He enumerated the accomplishments of his term of office but reminded his associates of what remained to be done—above all, the establishment of some kind of body to represent all active citizens, and, in pursuance of his ideal of national integration, a reform of the nobility that would deprive it of those privileges that separated it from the rest of the nation.

Marwitz's answer was that the reforms would surely compound the situation that had led to the collapse of 1806. To say that "the will of free men" was "the pillar of the state" was impressive as rhetoric, but did not hide the fact that broad grants of freedom to sections of the population that had shown neither patriotism nor loyalty nor discipline in 1806 were likely to undermine, rather than strengthen, the throne. The liberation of the peasants would not make them more likely to support the state, which they did not, in any case, understand; it would merely turn them against all authority. The national representation that Stein wanted would be employed by those represented for their own good, rather than the state's. As for the reform of the nobility, it seemed deliberately designed to destroy the one class that could be relied upon to fight against corrosive materialism and anarchy.

The last point was, of course, the most sensitive. Stein had no desire to destroy the nobility, but he did recognize in it an

12. F. A. L. von der Marwitz, *Aus dem Nachlasse,* 2 vols. (Berlin, 1852), II, 214.

obstacle to progressive reform. Of the East Elbian landowners, he asked: "What can we expect from the inhabitants of these sandy steppes—these artful, heartless, wooden, half-educated men, who are really capable only of becoming corporals or book-keepers?"[13] And, on another occasion: "The nobility of Prussia are a burden to the nation, because they are too numerous and for the most part poor and greedy for stipends, offices, privileges, and preferments of every kind. A consequence of their poverty is lack of education. . . . This mass of half-educated men [*Halbwisser*] exercize their presumption at the great expense of their fellow citizens in their double capacity as noblemen and officials."[14] There was no reason why this should be allowed to continue.

To Marwitz, on the other hand, the nobility had earned the privileges it possessed—its patrimonial rights at home, for example, and its access to high position in the state—by its sense of duty, its sense of honor, and its fortitude in time of trouble, all qualities proved in war, which was its special *métier* and for which the bourgeoisie and the intellectuals showed neither aptitude nor enthusiasm. Goethe, Marwitz once said after meeting him, was a good enough looking man but lacked "the natural grace of the nobleman" and the sense of honor that animated him. "Too much learning," Marwitz believed, "kills character." To talk about freedom while trampling on the rights of the one class that instinctively put duty before personal gain was to invite the utter downfall of Prussia.[15]

That the reformers were in fact intent on destroying that class seemed even more apparent to Marwitz when the Hardenberg government adopted a fiscal policy that imposed new burdens upon the landowning nobility and, in some cases, violated engagements made to them at the time of the coronation and oath

13. Ritter, *Stein,* pp. 382 f.
14. *Briefe und amtliche Schriften,* II, 853.
15. Fontane, *Sämtliche Werke,* X, 221. See also Kayser, *Marwitz,* pp. 184 f.

taking of Frederick William III. Claiming that this policy was a violation of the rights of the landed estate, Marwitz became the leader of a spirited opposition and wrote a series of violent memoranda for the king's eyes, culminating in a so-called Last Remonstrance (*Letzte Vorstellung*) in May 1811 in which, in the name of the landowners of Lebus and Beeskow-Storkow, he accused the government both of seeking to atomize the estates of the realm and create an undifferentiated mass of pliant subjects, and of trying to convert the owning of land to a purely economic function by depriving noble proprietors of their judicial and social functions and their collegial rights. The beneficiaries of this policy, he said, would be "the Jews who, already the undisputed masters of money, will now rise to become masters of the whole state," a barbed reference to Hardenberg's supposed predilection for Jewish fiscal advisors. The result of the mechanical leveling of all estates, he charged, "must necessarily be an attitude of general egoism and political irreligiosity, which regards the state as a mere agency of compulsion and takes the first opportunity to repudiate it in the hope of exercising power rather than suffering it. And that means Jacobin anarchy!"[16]

The remonstrance was directed against Hardenberg, but the real target was Stein, whom Marwitz regarded as the *spiritus rector* of a great plot against the real Prussia. He was later to write:

Stein began the revolutionizing of the fatherland, the war of the propertyless against property, of industry against agriculture, of the mob against the stable elements, of crass materialism against an order ordained by God, of expediency against law, of the present against the past and the future, of individuality against family, of speculation and the countinghouse against the fields and the trades, of bureaucracy against relationships rooted in the history of the land, of knowingness and imagined talent against virtue and honorable character. In this direction Stein seduced us, as if the embattled categories—property, agri-

16. Kayser, *Marwitz,* p. 226.

culture, stable relationships, the old order, law, community of estate members, and the principle of virtue and honor—were the causes of our fall![17]

In 1811, Hardenberg's response to the Last Remonstrance was to have Marwitz and an associate, Graf Finckenstein, arrested and imprisoned in Spandau fortress for "punishable criticism in disrespectful language of royal ordinances." The chancellor did this reluctantly and only because he felt that failure to discipline Marwitz in some way would damage the authority of the crown and jeopardize the whole of the reform movement that had begun in 1807. The action was, in fact, self-defeating. It made Marwitz a hero among his fellows, and it dramatized the opposition of the nobility to the attempts to modernize the state that Stein had begun and Hardenberg, with less energy, had continued. There is no doubt that this slowed the momentum of the reform movement, and the original pace was never again recovered, for in 1813 when Prussia went to war, the rebellious landowners were in the vanguard. Marwitz himself raised a militia regiment that acquitted itself well in a firefight near Hagelberg in 1813; he was attached to Blücher's army in the battles of Ligny and Wevre, came out of the war as a colonel, and was promoted to general in 1817. The war put the noble landowners back in the saddle in more than the literal sense, for they triumphed, not only over Napoleon, but over Stein as well. When they rode home, the shame of Jena had been forgotten; the old Prussia had rehabilitated itself; and the last of the reformers were soon forced from office.

IV

This development came as no surprise to Stein. He said bitterly that Marwitz and his associates were "prejudiced, egotistical

17. Marwitz, *Aus dem Nachlasse,* I, 292.

Halbwisser—a crowd of malicious or stupid ranters, who don't want to carry the burdens that necessity has imposed,"[18] but he was under no illusion about their influence. In 1812 and 1813, when Prussian policy seemed to be repeating the hesitant pre-Jena course, he tended to agree with Gneisenau's bitter judgment —"We will go under with shame, for we dare not hide from ourselves that the nation is as bad as its government."[19] As far as he could see, from his perhaps skewed perspective in Russian headquarters, the reform had failed, and he had no great expectations for Prussia in the impending crisis. Indeed, he virtually disassociated himself from his adopted country in that often-quoted letter to his friend Ernst Graf von Münster in which he wrote:

> I am sorry that you detect the Prussian in me. . . . I have only one fatherland, and that is Germany, and since, according to the old constitution, I belonged only to it and not to any separate part of it, so now I give my whole being only to it and not to a part of it.[20]

Even in his defeat, if the incomplete realization of his hopes can be called that, Stein remained a formidable figure in German politics, the symbol of hope that Prussia might still enter upon the road that the countries of western Europe had taken, the father of a new German liberalism, whose "testament" was remembered and reprinted whenever the forces of movement seemed to be stirring again. But perhaps, in the context of lectures entitled "The End of Prussia," Marwitz was the more significant figure of the two. It is perhaps worth noting that in his last years he was taken up by the crown prince, the later Frederick William IV, and cultivated and honored. This was appropriate enough. In his own way, he was a predecessor of

18. Ritter, *Stein*, p. 383.
19. Ibid.
20. *Briefe und amtliche Schriften*, III, 818.

the camarilla of 1848, the agrarian politicians of the *Bund der Landwirte* in the 1890s, and the circle of aristocratic landowners who surrounded President von Hindenburg at Neudeck in 1932 and 1933. He was, in many ways, a nobler person than the Manteuffels and Hammersteins and Oldenburg-Januschaus, but *autres temps, autres moeurs.* He in his time, as they in theirs, was an all-too-effective opponent of the new, and hence a harbinger of the end of Prussia.

CHAPTER 2

Romance and Reality:
Bettina von Arnim and Bismarck

In his memoirs, Otto von Bismarck had occasion to talk of his old antagonist in the diplomatic battles of the '70s, the Russian foreign minister Prince Gorchakov: "Of Gorchakov," he wrote, "his subordinates in the ministry said: *'Il se mire dans son encrier'* [He admires himself in his inkwell.]" And then Bismarck added, "In analogous fashion, Bettina said of her brother-in-law, the famous Savigny, 'He can't step across a puddle without using it as a looking glass.'"[1]

This afterthought must have puzzled some of the chancellor's readers, whose recollection of Bettina von Arnim, who died in 1859, could not have been very clear; and it was, in any case, a curious flashback in time, from the world of the '90s, in which Bismarck was writing, and that of the Congress of Berlin, of which he was writing, to the world of the '40s, that of Frederick William IV and the Young German movement, when Bettina was the most-talked-about woman in Berlin and he himself an ambitious young politician. But it is not unnatural for old men to have sudden recollections of their youth and to remember people who were part of it; and although it does not appear that Bismarck ever actually met Bettina, he may have remembered her with affection, not only because of her mali-

1. Otto von Bismarck, *Gedanken und Erinnerungen* (new ed., Stuttgart, 1928), p. 420.

cious humor, but because he recognized a certain temperamental affinity with her. In 1868 the novelist Gustav Freytag described Bismarck as a not untypical product of the '40s, in spirit closer to the Young German movement than to either the romantics or the esthetes of the aristocracy like the Humboldts, "[with] a lack of reverence, a tendency to regard everything capriciously and from a personal point of view, and, at the same time, . . . a vital energy that is fresh and impudent."[2] A telling description of Bismarck, but no less so of Bettina von Arnim, who, as we shall see, was as irreverent, as capricious, as self-centered, and as energetic as he.

Nor was this the only similarity. If I am wrong in thinking that the old chancellor may have recognized a psychological kinship with Bettina, he would certainly have remembered that, in those now distant days of his youth, Bettina and he had, albeit very indirectly, been rival claimants for the right to chart Prussia's future. In the circle surrounding Frederick William IV, where the political decisions of that time were made, they were important, even if subordinate, figures. Indeed, in some ways, they were the most interesting actors in the play to catch the conscience of the king.

I

In Prussian history, the 1840s are remembered as a decade that opened with high hopes and ended in disappointment and a failed revolution. The accession to the throne in 1840 of a vigorous and supposedly progressive ruler seemed to herald an end to the years of reaction that had followed the departure from office of the last of Stein's associates in 1819 and to promise that a new era of reform and movement toward constitutional government was about to begin; and the new monarch encour-

2. *Gustav Freytags Briefe an Albrecht von Stosch* (Leipzig, 1913), 24 September 1868.

aged these expectations by bringing into his entourage men of enlightened views like Hermann von Boyen and Alexander von Humboldt. But from the beginning there was skepticism about what all this portended, and the extraordinary performance of the king at the ceremonies of homage (*Huldigung*) that accompanied his assumption of the throne did nothing to relieve it.

In the *Huldigung* in Berlin, Frederick William stood before the crowd of fifty to sixty thousand people who had assembled between the royal palace and the museum and cried:

> Noblemen! Burghers! People from the land! and from the uncounted hosts, all! All who can hear my voice, I ask you: Will you, with heart and spirit, with word and deed, and in all your striving in the sacred loyalty of the Germans [*Teutschen*] and in the even more sacred love of Christians, help and stand by me in order to maintain Prussia as it is . . . and as it must remain, if it is not to perish? Will you help and stand by me in the effort to develop even more gloriously those qualities that have made Prussia, with its mere fourteen million people, one of the great powers of the earth? Then answer me with the clearest, most beautiful sound in our mother tongue, answer me with a firm and honorable Yes!

And when the throng had responded the orator continued:

> Your Yes was for me—it is my own—I shall not relinquish it— it binds us, with bonds that cannot be loosed, in mutual love and loyalty. That gives me courage, strength, comfort! That will I not forget in the hour of my death! I will keep the vow that I made to you, here and in Königsberg, so help me God! In witness I raise my right hand to heaven! Now bring this sublime ceremony to its conclusion! And may the fructifying blessing of God rest upon this hour![3]

Even in the age of the Biedermeier, when orotundity was not uncommon, this speech was very odd. The talk of main-

---

3. Walter Bussmann, *Wandel und Kontinuität in Politik und Geschichte* (Boppard, 1973), pp. 298 f.

taining Prussia as it was was daunting to anyone who hoped for change, and the rhetoric evoked, not the future, but the past. Indeed, the speech was a blend of bogus medievalism and the kind of *Deutschtümelei* or archaic Germanomania that Heinrich Heine mocked in the fourth book of his essay on Ludwig Börne which came out in this same year. The ceremony of homage revealed that the king was a romantic, captivated by pictures of a past that never existed and had no relevance to contemporary issues and aspirations; and this impression was confirmed in the years that followed. About the king's love for his people there was no doubt, but he had no feeling for their problems, and therefore his undeniable artistic talents and his religiosity soon alienated them. He became the butt of some of Heine's more unpleasant poems and of the Young German Adolf Glassbrenner's outrageous lampoons in his series *Berlin as It Lives and Drinks.* Varnhagen von Ense, in his informative diary, reported the wide currency of jokes about his unworldliness (*Weltfremdheit*) and his dilettantism. The king reacted to these gibes with irritation and withdrawal, with the repeal of the civil liberties and the press freedom that he had tolerated at the outset of his reign, and with a deepening political conservatism. The course was thus set for a revolution which— because the country was not really prepared for it when it came —was a failure and led to a further period of the kind of sterile reaction from which Prussia seemed fated never to escape.

Into this situation, Bettina von Arnim and Bismarck came as realists intent on breaking the spell of the king's romantic enchantment with the past and turning his eyes to the future.

To call Bettina a realist would seem to be a willful denial of the extent to which she was herself a product of the romantic period. The granddaughter of Sophie de la Roche, the friend of Wieland, and herself the author of sentimental novels, she was the sixth of eight gifted and eccentric children of an Italian import dealer who lived in Frankfurt am Main and a German mother whose beauty had attracted the attention of the young Goethe. Bettina's older brother Clemens was a poet of considerable power, a collector of folk songs, and the author of fairytales (like "The Tale of Gockel and Hinkel") and some of the most influential stories of the romantic period, like the death-laden "History of True Kasperl and Beautiful Annerl." Clemens not only guided his sister's reading but introduced her to his friends and acquaintances in the arts, and she soon became spoiled, precocious, and self-centered, given to bizarre language and strange conceits. "My soul is a passionate dancer," she wrote to her brother. "She dances to hidden music which only I can hear. You may tell me to be calm and demure, but my soul does not listen and goes on dancing; if the dance were to stop, it would be the end of me. I trust the elements in myself that want to kick over the traces."[4]

It was at Clemens's suggestion that, at the age of fifteen, she read Goethe's *Wilhelm Meister*, in consequence of which, and perhaps because of her knowledge of her mother's abortive affair with its author she became obsessed with the poet. She began to think of herself as Mignon, the mysterious child whom Goethe/Meister saves from the acrobats and who subsequently falls in love with him. Like Mignon, she began to strike exotic attitudes and to sleep with her hands folded on her breast. She made friends with Goethe's mother, who lived in Frankfurt, and could not rest until she had met the poet himself, which she succeeded in doing in 1807, thereafter bombarding him with a stream of letters filled with her dreams and enthusiasms and with demands and admonitions and declarations of love that must have bewildered and perhaps exhausted the sage of Weimar, who was already fifty-eight years old when Bettina burst upon him. She had a similarly emotional correspondence with

4. Arthur Helps and Elizabeth Jane Howard, *Bettina: A Portrait* (New York, n.d.), p. 33.

Karoline von Günderode, a poetess who finally committed suicide in a suitably romantic manner because she was disappointed in love, and with Ludwig van Beethoven, whose stature she, with her brother and E. T. A. Hoffmann, recognized sooner than most contemporaries and with whom, in long intimate letters, she discussed the electrical qualities of music and its power to dissolve the barriers between souls.

In a letter to Goethe's mother, Bettina wrote, "I really belong to the period of the extreme romantics, and I should have been a character in *Werther* and would have been turned out of doors by Lotte."[5] But, if this was true, it was also true that, even when she was young, her emotional transports were always balanced by a strong satirical sense and the gift of self-mockery. Writing to her sister Gunda about a letter from Goethe, she could say:

> I have been so happy since I got this letter that the most terrible disaster might befall me and I would not notice it. Adieu, my friend and sharer of my joys, adieu, Gundel — [you want] 2 wursts, 3 lbs. noodles, ¼ cwt. candles, but what do you think? this very moment I have got a second letter from Goethe: it is incredible, a storm of blessed lightning strikes the house: the flames leap up over my head, and I do not move but burn with joy and enthusiasm: the ashes go with the wind, the spirit hies itself to Abraham's bosom or wherever it likes, but why does Gundel want such a quantity of noodles? I can't stand them.[6]

The romantic was, in fact, quite capable of dealing with such mundane things as noodles and candles and, when she married Achim von Arnim, who had been her brother's collaborator in the collection of folk songs called *Des Knaben Wunderhorn,* she proved to be a loving wife and helpmate for twenty years, bearing seven children and managing Arnim's estate at Wiepersdorf

5. Ibid., p. 81.
6. Ibid., p. 87.

and his house in Berlin with efficiency. Moreover, when her husband died in 1831, she did not hesitate to direct her old romanticism into practical channels, by writing two letter-novels, *Goethe's Correspondence with a Child* and *The Günderode,* that made her famous and left her reasonably well off.

In her youth, Bettina had once written, "What is the use of all my energy and enterprise if I have no means of applying it? I feel like a warrior who longs to do great deeds but who lies in prison laden with chains with no hope of rescue."[7] This feeling of frustration had been relieved by her marriage, by her acquaintance with Goethe, and by her tribute to his memory, which was published, it should be remembered, at a time when his reputation was in decline and when it had become fashionable to denigrate his achievement. But what was she to do now that her debt to Goethe was discharged and her husband dead?

The answer was that she began to turn her attention to politics. Her house became a gathering place for the new political and cultural opposition to the government, a place where one might meet liberals of the 1813 generation like Varnhagen and Alexander von Humboldt, members of the reviving *Burschenschaft* movement (Bettina dedicated her Günderode book to the student generation), and radical writers of the Young German movement like Karl Gutzkow and Ludolf Wienbarg. Her salon was as famous as Rahel Levin's had once been and more oriented to contemporary political issues upon which Bettina did not hesitate to declare herself. She became, indeed, a force in liberal politics, and there was nothing adventitious about this. She had always been a free spirit and a believer in engagement, and even in her youth her brother had written a poem to her in which he said that everything that was touched by her creative spirit was awakened to a new life of freedom:

7. Ibid., p. 37.

Alles Bettine! dem liebend Dein schaffender Geist
   sich genährt,
Was Deine segnende Hand, was Dein Gedanke berührt,
Blühet schöner ein Freiheit verklärendes Leben.[8]

An early instance of her new political engagement came in
1839. Two years earlier, seven professors of the University of
Göttingen had been dismissed from their posts by the king of
Hannover because they refused to break their oaths to a constitution that he had abrogated. Two of them, the philologists
and folklorists Jakob and Wilhelm Grimm, who were members
of the Prussian Academy, hoped to find posts in Prussia but
received no support, either from the academy's president, Karl
Lachmann, or from Karl Savigny, an intimate advisor of the
king, both of whom justified their position with contrived political and legal arguments. This enraged Bettina, and she ad-
dressed a long letter to Savigny, who was her brother-in-law,
with a copy to the king. She pointed out that the case of the
Grimms might seem, as Savigny had intimated, too trivial to
be brought to the government's attention, and yet the grand
duke of Weimar had not hesitated to open his borders to the
expelled professors. It was necessary, she wrote pointedly, for
Prussia to do the same. "One can act greatly even in trivial things,
but that which cries to heaven is never trivial."

Then in a passage that pointed to the future, Bettina wrote:

> I know you wouldn't say this to the king, for to tell a prince
> about the mistakes his government makes or to show him a
> more elevated point of view would be contrary to the politics
> of respect. . . . You treat princes like automata. . . . You make
> to them only the speeches they are able to answer without wak-
> ing up, for the truth would waken them, and they wouldn't

8. Clemens Brentano, *Gedichte,* ed. Wolfgang Frühwald, Bernhard Gajek und
Friedhelm Kemp (Munich, 1977), p. 76.

be automata any more, but independent rulers, and reason of state would no longer be bound up with baseness, but would be transformed into world wisdom, which comes from God's wisdom.[9]

This passage helps to explain Bettina's attitude and behavior once Frederick William IV had become king. When the high hopes that had attended his accession began to fade, she became convinced that he was in the hands of evil counsellors. As she was to write later:

Ah! the evil intrigues that encircle the lofty spirit of a prince, until the nobility of his soul is wounded to death and a woeful tragedy is performed . . . in which his retainers exude a fog of lies about him and no hero of the truth [*Wahrheitsheld*] is present to master this evil.[10]

More than most princes, Frederick William needed a *Wahrheitsheld,* and Bettina nominated herself for that position.

This could be described as a quixotic and essentially romantic notion, and Werner Vordtriede has explained it by saying that, in contrast to her brother Clemens, Bettina had foresworn Christianity but always needed a God on earth who could be father, friend, lover, and companion and that Frederick William was her substitute for Goethe, who had filled those roles. This wholly overlooks the fact that the king's chosen counsellors *were* bad counsellors, caught as they were in the romantic conservatism of the post-1815 period, and that Bettina's advice for the king was in no wise romantic but focused on some hard realities that were being generally overlooked. In her role as self-appointed royal advisor, she continued to call the king's attention to injustice

9. Hellmut Kühn and Manfred Schlösser, "Bettina von Arnim: Ein Brief," in *Preussen, Dein Spree-Athen,* ed. Hellmut Kühn (Hamburg, 1981), pp. 98 ff.

10. Werner Vordtriede, *Bettina von Arnims Armenbuch* (Frankfurt am Main, 1981), p. 123.

to individuals, to breaches of civil liberties, to restrictions on thought and expression; but the center of her attention—and here she was certainly among the clearest-eyed of her generation —was the evils generated by the new industrialism.

As early as 1831, when she risked her life to bring relief to the victims of the cholera epidemic, Bettina had become aware of the misery and squalor of the area outside the Hamburger Gate in Berlin, an industry-created slum called the Vogtland. In the '40s, she often visited it with friends, and there is a story, doubtless apocryphal, that on one occasion her companion was a young man called Karl Marx. In 1842, when she published a curious work which she called *This Book Belongs to the King*, she included at the end a collection of case studies of poverty in the Vogtland, an unprecedented little sociological study of the results of industrialism. The text of the King's Book, as it was called, was largely cast in the form of a series of discussions between Goethe's mother, a parson, and a *Bürgermeister*, in the course of which Goethe's mother, speaking for Bettina, placed the blame for these conditions upon the orthodox church and the bureaucracy.

The book might have had little effect. It was difficult to read; the king professed to be baffled by it; and after reading it a young poet named Theodor Fontane, who will concern us later in these lectures, wrote a poem to Bettina in which he said that her spirit was like a lark ascending to heaven but that, unfortunately, it often disappeared behind clouds that were impenetrable to ordinary humans:

> *Dein Geist nimmt, wie auf Lerchenschwingen,*
> *Tief in den Himmel seinen Zug,*
> *Und freudig lausch' ich seinem Singen*
> *Und freudig folg' ich seinem Flug.*
>
> *Doch wie die Lerch' auf ihren Zügen*
> *Oftmals im Äther mir verschwimmt,*

So auch dein Geist auf seinen Flügen,
Wenn er zu hoch ins Blaue klimmt.[11]

But government heavy-handedness saved it. When a shortened version was prepared by Bettina's friend Adolf Stahr, it was seized by the authorities, which of course advertised it and inspired imitation. Adolf Glassbrenner wrote a poignant *Petition to the King* which purported to be from "ein janz armer Mann, der nicht weis, wo er Haupt hinkriechen soll"[12] ("a very poor man who doesn't know where he can lay his head") and there were other experiments in this genre. Moreover, Bettina was herself encouraged to more systematic effort. She appealed to the press for information about poverty in other parts of Prussia, intending to publish it in an *Armenbuch* (Book of the Poor). In its original form, this plan had to be abandoned, again because of government intervention. Bettina was, indeed, getting on officialdom's nerves, and a widely publicized remark of hers to the effect that the king's enthusiasm for completing the long-delayed construction of Cologne Cathedral was misplaced and that it would do more good if he built it in Silesia and gave employment to the people of that distressed area led to furious charges from the ministry of the interior that she was inciting to riot. She was, in fact, held responsible for the subsequent rising of the Silesian weavers in 1846, an event that shocked the nation and seemed to portend the kind of collapse that came in 1848. During the revolution of that year, Bettina was under surveillance, and her pen was still. It was only after the revolution was over and reaction was setting in again that she returned stubbornly to her fixed idea and tried for the last time to talk with the king, this time in an even

11. "An Bettina" in Theodor Fontane, *Sämtliche Werke*, Nymphenburg ed., XX (Munich, 1962), p. 633.
12. Adolf Glassbrenner, *Der politisierende Eckensteher,* ed. Jost Hermand (Stuttgart, 1969), pp. 74f.

more turgid and largely unread book called *Conversation with Demons.*

It is clear, from sketches that Bettina made for the exordium of the unwritten *Armenbuch,* and from the strange dialogues between the author and the sleeping king in the new book, that Bettina did not know what caused poverty and, indeed, appeared at times to regard it as a form of damnation that had no rational cause and could be solved only by a general spiritual regeneration. What she was sure of was that the country could not survive this evil. She recognized, sooner than most, that the social problem was the real problem of the future and necessarily the government's first priority. And by the government, she meant the king. Between him and his people there was indeed — as Frederick William had sensed in his homage ceremonies — a mystical bond that made him the people's natural leader. If he refused to allow false counsellors to mislead him, if he was ever conscious of the problems of the poor, the fourth and most vulnerable estate of his realm, if he granted them their proper share in the nation's affairs, so that their voice was heard and their advice considered, the result could only be national integration and social peace. But first the king must awaken and seek his natural allies.

If all this seems too simple to be practical (Heinrich Heine, for one, thought it was and in one of his verses said that the very idea that Bettina might be taken seriously was a sign that the world was turned upside down), it should be remembered that, at a later time, when the nation was riven by class discord and political disorientation, a not unsophisticated man, Friedrich Naumann, returned to the essence of Bettina's idea in his *Demokratie und Kaisertum,* in which he saw a firm alliance between crown and people as the alternative to social chaos. But we need not dwell upon the question of practicality. Bettina's realism lay in pointing out that the world had changed and no longer resembled the one that captivated the imagination of the king and his counsellors, and that the new industrialism and its social effects were the problem that had to be dealt with if Prussia was to become a sound and progressive state. As she once wrote:

> The poor should be able to have a share in public affairs, for the legislators would then acquire sounder views about citizenship and public welfare. Since the poor are a fourth, and indeed the greatest, estate, why are they not represented by deputies? . . . The interests of the other three estates must yield to that of this fourth estate. Cities have property; the land has property; rulers have property and thrive on it. Why has poverty no property? The poor, deprived of their rights, are citizens who are too weak to protect themselves. One can find protection for public freedom only where the true power is. We are not in a position to be free except with the people and through the people.[13]

II

Otto von Bismarck was a different kind of realist. Like Bettina, he recognized that the world had changed, in ways beyond the comprehension of his class and party, but the prescription that he had to offer for the future was not a policy of domestic concern and social reconciliation but rather one of skillful maneuver in the world of international politics and the cold and unsentimental search for power. It is part of the tragedy of Prussia —indeed, it was another long step toward the end of Prussia— that his policy rather than Bettina's was in the long run adopted.

Like Bettina, Bismarck's early life had a distinctly romantic coloration. In 1839, having terminated a brief career as a fledgling civil servant with the vow that he would "make the kind of music I like or none at all"[14] and decided to live the life of

13. Vordtriede, *Armenbuch,* pp. 71 f.
14. Otto von Bismarck, *Briefe an seine Frau und Gattin,* ed. Fürst Herbert Bismarck (Stuttgart, 1900), p. 27.

the simple *Landjunker* on his estate at Kniephof, he entered into
the same Christian-German circle that fed the archaic notions
of Frederick William IV and his chosen advisors the Gerlachs
and the Manteuffels. This was reflected not only in his personal
life (his emotional problems, religious conversion, and court-
ship) but in the style and argument of the speeches that he made
when he went, as representative of his estate, to the meeting
of the United Landtag in 1847. And what could have been more
like a chapter in a romantic novel than his reaction to the outbreak of the revolution in March 1848 — his arming his peasants
for a possible march upon the rebellious capital, the elaborate
mystagogery of his secret visits to Berlin and Potsdam, dressed
in a slouched hat with a bright cockade and with his beard shaved
off to disguise him from the mob, and his attempts to persuade
the army commanders to disobey their orders and rescue the
king against his will?

It was Bismarck's attitude in 1848 and the memory of his
speeches in the United Landtag that commended him to the
conservative party and the king's *ministère occulte,* who saw in
him a Marwitz *redivivus,* a defender of the old Prussia, who was
perhaps a bit too extreme in his public statements but who could,
nevertheless, be relied on. This was, of course, a fundamental
misreading of his character and thought. It was only when he
was an old man and saw his life work threatened that Bismarck
became a conservative like the Gerlachs and the king's camarilla. When he was young, despite his occasional antique attitudes and his apparent reverence for tradition, he always had
a sense of the inevitability of change and a confidence, which
grew with the years, in his ability to exploit it for his own advantage. It was not for nothing that the Latin tag *rebus sic stantibus* was often in his mouth, for, despite appearances, he was
not a man of fixed principles but always recognized that circumstances alter cases. Above all, he knew that the events of
the late '40s had changed politics in a fundamental way, that

new methods would be needed and new courses tried. He said as much in his first speech to the Prussian chamber after the outbreak of the revolution, in words that still echoed his bitterness over the king's capitulation. "The past is buried, and I regret it more painfully than many of you that no human power is in a position to bring it to life again, after the crown itself has thrown earth upon the coffin."[15]

It was not often that Bismarck could be as frank as that. After he had decided to become a professional politician, in February 1849, when he was elected to the new Prussian Landtag for the electoral district Zauche-Belzig-Brandenburg and had resolved to lease his estate and move his family to Berlin, he needed the support and protection of the extreme right, without which he would have had no political base at all. He found it expedient to support their positions and to argue their cases and, indeed, since on the whole he agreed with their basic stance in politics, did so gladly enough. But he was not nearly as much their man as he appeared, and as Friedrich Meinecke was the first to point out, this was apparent, although not widely appreciated at the time, as soon as he began to talk about foreign policy.

As the revolution in Germany reached its height at the beginning of 1849, the national assembly in Frankfurt, having drawn up a constitution for all Germany, offered the imperial title to the Prussian king. Frederick William refused the offer with contempt, because it had been made by representatives of the people rather than by his equals, but he could, nevertheless, not put the idea out of his mind. He had always been an enthusiast for German unity, although his view was colored by romanticism. His dreams were of renewing state and society in the spirit of Christianity by the reconstitution of the Holy Roman Em-

15. Lothar Gall, *Bismarck, der weisse Revolutionär* (Frankfurt am Main, 1980), p. 75.

pire; and, under the influence of a Catholic advisor, Joseph Maria von Radowitz, he embarked upon a scheme to bring the princes of northern Germany together in a league under Prussian leadership that would be the first step toward a wider union with Austria that would reestablish the old Reich.

At this time in his life, Bismarck regarded the question of German unity without enthusiasm (in his *burschikos* manner, he said it was a swindle perpetrated by liberal parliamentarians to drown Prussia in a sea of South German *Gemütlichkeit*); and he viewed Radowitz with the same suspicion that Bettina had for the king's domestic advisors, as a false counsellor, or, as he once said, as "the clever cloakroom attendant for the king's medieval fantasy."[16] He therefore intervened actively in the offensive against the so-called Prussian Union that was launched by the conservatives. But, whereas Julius Stahl, the theorist of the extreme right, attacked the scheme because it would reinflame the spirit of revolution in Germany, Bismarck's argument was based almost exclusively, not on ideological grounds, but upon the questions of interest and power. From the Prussian point of view, he asked in his first major foreign policy speech on 6 September 1849, what was to be gained from the completion of the plan? Its proponents promised only intangibles, whereas in reality the plan threatened to make Prussia the tool of lesser powers, and it would have been rejected for that reason alone by a ruler like Frederick the Great. Indeed, had Frederick been alive, he would have recognized only two logical policies for Prussia after the refusal of the imperial crown, either "to join with the old battle comrade Austria . . . in order to destroy the common enemy revolution. Or . . . to tell the Germans, under the threat of throwing the sword into the balance, what their constitution should be. The latter would be a national Prussian policy. Thus, Prussia would gain, in the one case through union

16. Bismarck, *Gedanken und Erinnerungen*, p. 89.

with Austria, in the other through herself alone, the right position from which to help Germany to the power that it deserves in Europe."

This was an entirely new kind of language, and the most striking aspect of the speech was that Bismarck gave no intimation of which of the two policies he preferred. That would be determined, he intimated, by the *rebus sic stantibus,* or by chance. "In the long run or the short," Bismarck declared, "the God who rules the battlefields must throw the iron dice of decision."[17]

If this was uncomfortable doctrine for the king and Radowitz, with their dreams of a restored medieval empire, it was no more palatable to those who opposed the union plan on ideological grounds and wished to return to a firm conservative alliance with Austria and Russia. Nor was the language of Bismarck's speech in the chamber in December 1850, when the union plan had led to a major crisis with Austria and war was at stake:

I would not shrink back from this war, indeed, I would advise it, if anyone was in a position to prove to me that it was necessary or show me a worthy objective that would be attained by it and could not be won without war. Why do great states fight wars these days? The only sound basis for a great state, and this is what differentiates it from a small one, is stately egoism and not romanticism, and it is not worthy of a great state to fight for a cause that has nothing to do with its own interest. Therefore, gentlemen, show me an objective worthy of war, and I will vote with you. It is easy for a statesman, whether in the cabinet or in the chamber, to go with the popular mood and blow into the war trumpet and then to warm himself by the fireplace or make thundering speeches at this tribune and to leave it to the musketeer, who bleeds in the snow, whether his system brings victory and shame. There is nothing easier than that. But woe to the statesman who does not at this time

17. Horst Kohl, ed. *Die politischen Reden des Fürsten Bismarck, 1847–1897,* 14 vols. (Stuttgart, 1892–1905), I, 103 ff.

look out for a reason for war that will stand the test when the war is done.[18]

The whole of the later Bismarck is in that speech—the style, the personality, the philosophy of peace and war. But, leaving that aside, I think we can regard this speech and the earlier one of September 1849 as the beginning of Bismarck's private campaign to free the king and his advisors from romanticism and to convince them that only the most rigorous and unsentimental attention to considerations of interest and power would assure Prussia's survival in the uncertain situation that followed the revolutions of 1848. And in the 1850s, when Bismarck was serving as Prussia's representative at the federal diet in Frankfurt, he continued his effort to persuade and convert. That was the spirit behind both his correspondence with Leopold von Gerlach, who was always close to the seat of power, and the remarkable dispatches that he sent to the foreign ministry. The calm insistence with which the young diplomat argued that there were no permanent friends or foes in foreign policy shocked the ears of some of his auditors, as did the not infrequent brutality of his proposals:

> Sympathies and antipathies with respect to foreign powers and persons I cannot justify to my sense of duty to the foreign service of my country, either in myself or in others. Therein lies the embryo of disloyalty toward . . . the land one serves. . . . Not even the king has the right to subordinate the interests of the fatherland to personal feelings of love and hatred toward the foreigner.[19]

When he recommended a bold policy in German affairs, since "fear and more fear is the only thing that has an effect in the residences of Munich and Bückeburg," Leopold von Gerlach remonstrated that "even a good cause did not justify evil ac-

18. Kohl, *Reden*, I, 261 ff.
19. Bismarck, *Gesammelte Werke*, XIV/1, 465.

tions." Bismarck was not abashed and answered cheekily, "It is better to save oneself by means of a sewer than to let oneself be beaten or strangled."[20]

Once the Crimean War had hopelessly split the great powers and left Austria in a state of embarrassed isolation, Bismarck's thinking became more militant and began to turn upon the necessity of Prussia's exploiting Austria's difficulties, and even going to war against Austria should a favorable opportunity present itself. In the so-called Splendid Dispatch (*Prachtbericht*) of 26 April 1856, in which he surveyed the current state of Europe, there was a significant passage that was—as Lothar Gall has recently pointed out—very bad history but interesting for the light it throws on Bismarck's thinking: "The German dualism has for a thousand years intermittently, and since Charles V regularly every century, regulated its reciprocal relationship by a thorough internal war, and in this century too no other means than this will be able to set the clock of evolution at its proper hour."[21] When he wrote those words, Bismarck was only a chief of mission, trying from his post abroad to educate the king and his associates in the realities of politics. But it was not difficult to guess, from reading the *Prachtbericht*, what kind of course he would chart if he were ever given the authority to make the decisions by himself; and only six years after he wrote that dispatch—to be sure, under a different king—he was in that position.

III

One can imagine what Bettina would have sought to do had she been given the opportunity that came to Bismarck in September 1862. Back in 1844, someone had sent her a notice about a weaver in Langenbielau who had strangled his two-year-old

20. See Gall, *Bismarck,* pp. 169–72.
21. Bismarck, *Gesammelte Werke,* II, 142.

child and then hanged himself because he had no employment and no food. On the notice, someone had written, "I would not like to be the king of Prussia!" Bettina's comment was, "But I *would* like to be . . . and how can I comfort myself that I am not? When so many great things could be done through me! When I could lift the evil spell from the world and lay the foundation of a paradise far greater and more powerful and heaven-aspiring than all the great powers!"[22]

Bismarck's thoughts were closer to earth, focused indeed upon the great powers that Bettina scorned and Prussia's place among them rather than upon the problems that concerned her and the policy of reconciliation that she proposed for their solution. "The eyes of Germany," he told the budget commission of the Landtag, in the speech for which he is best remembered, "are not on Prussia's liberalism but on her armed might. . . . The great questions of the day are decided . . . by iron and blood."[23]

This was language that outraged both liberals and conservatives, although Bismarck's right-wing allies may have comforted themselves with that piece of German folk wisdom that holds that the soup is not eaten as hot as it is cooked. But as the months and years passed and the new minister's policy unfolded, his demonic unconditionality became apparent, and it was clear that he would be restrained by neither the precepts of conventional morality nor the traditions of Prussian policy. He was, in fact, intent upon an increase of power that could only be at the expense of Prussia's Austrian ally, his aim an enhanced role in European politics that would launch Prussia upon uncharted seas. When they realized this, a significant part of the old Prussian conservative party shrank back in consternation from what they openly called Bismarck's delusions of grandeur (*Grössenwahn*). In May 1866, when he had brought the country

22. Vordtriede, *Armenbuch*, pp. 67f.
23. Kohl, *Reden*, II, 30.

to the verge of war with Austria, Ernst Ludwig von Gerlach, writing in the *Neue Preussische Zeitung*, finally broke with a policy that seemed to him to be immoral and potentially disastrous, and Bismarck's old friend Reinhold von Thadden-Trieglaff (the great-grandfather of the historian whom I quoted in my first lecture) wrote to congratulate him on his article, in words that Professor Hamerow has quoted with effect in the second volume of his *Social Foundations of German Unification*:

> By your article you have performed a service to your party beyond description. We were already at the point of going rashly with the ministry through thick and thin and turning into downright Bonapartists. We had already abandoned all moral foundations or ceased to care about them, so that your waking call and warning cry were very timely. Surrendering completely to the sweet lust of acquisition, we already considered ourselves entirely free of the obligation to reflect, until your voice pierced the dull confusion.[24]

But it was, in fact, already too late for reflection. The momentum of events proved irreversible, and within two months Prussia was at war with Austria and the battle of Königgrätz was fought and won. After that there was a new mood throughout the land that showed all too clearly that the policy of power had triumphed. The question now was whether Prussia, which might have profited from Bettina von Arnim's realism, could survive Bismarck's.

24. Theodore S. Hamerow, *The Social Foundations of German Unification, 1858– 1871*: II. *Struggles and Accomplishments* (Princeton, 1972), p. 255.

CHAPTER 3

The Triumph of Borussismus:
Theodor Fontane and William II

On 17 January 1871, the day before he was to be proclaimed
as emperor of the new German Reich in the Hall of Mirrors
in Versailles, King William I of Prussia said to his minister president, "Tomorrow will be the unhappiest day of my life. For
we will be carrying the kingdom of Prussia to its grave, and
you, Prince Bismarck, will be responsible for that."[1]

When we think of the constitutional and political circumstances of the German Empire of 1871–1918, it is difficult to
regard this as anything but the testy remark of a tired old man
who was bewildered by the complexities of the situation at the
end of the war with France. After all, in the new federal organization of Germany, Prussia was as clearly the hegemonial power
as it had been in the North German Confederation after 1866.
It was by far the largest of the member states in territory, population, and social product; it had a virtual monopoly of military
power, since there was no imperial army, and even those states
like Bavaria, Württemberg, and Baden that retained military
establishments of their own were bound to the Prussian army
by conventions that indicated how illusory their independence
was. Politically too it was supreme, because its power in the
federal council was so great that it could block any proposed

1. Hermann Oncken, *Grossherzog Friedrich I von Baden,* 2 vols. (Stuttgart, 1927),
I, 326.

legislation that seemed to threaten its interest. From 1871 to 1917, every Reich chancellor, with the exception of Hohenlohe, was a Prussian; the administrative offices of the Reich were staffed predominantly by Prussian bureaucrats; directives of the Prussian state ministry determined important aspects of federal policy; and laws passed by the Prussian Landtag affected the circumstances of citizens in the greater part of the Reich. None of this corroborated the king's doleful prognostications.

And yet, in a deeper sense, he was right. In that too exuberant, too boastful, too flashy ceremony in the Hall of Mirrors, something of the old essence of Prussia did give up the ghost, and in the years that followed the values that had characterized the kingdom of Frederick William I and Frederick II were subverted by those of the new age of materialism and power. If the success of Bismarck's policies in the '60s produced an enlarged Prussia, it also resulted in a new Prussianism, which assumed its most objectionable and dangerous form under the reign of Emperor William II. This so-called *Borussismus,* or *Borussianismus,* was once defined by one of Bismarck's staunchest opponents, the great Catholic bishop of Mainz, Wilhelm Emanuel Freiherr von Ketteler:

> By *Borussianismus,* we understand an *idée fixe* about Prussia's calling, a vague conception of a world mission imposed on Prussia, tied up with the conviction that this calling and task are absolutely necessary ones . . . and that it is impermissible to oppose [them] in the name of law or history. . . . The nature of the calling differs greatly in accordance with the position of those who believe in it. If a man is a dedicated servant of his king, then he thinks of the supremacy of an absolute Prussian monarchy; if he is a soldier, he thinks of a Prussian military state with its warlord; if he is a bureaucrat, of the glorification of the Prussian bureaucracy; if he is a preacher, of the spread of Protestantism under the leadership of the Prussian kingdom. . . . But, however different their views may be, they make of them a fixed idea of a Prussian calling. . . . *Borussianismus* is thus

doctrinairism of the highest degree; it is an abstract system and therefore, in a real sense, an arbitrary form of fantasy.[2]

Despite the heady excitement that accompanied the victories over Austria and France and the subsequent establishment of the Reich (*Reichsgründung*), there were many Germans who had doubts about the future. Those who expressed them forcefully were, to be sure, fewer in number and generally non-Prussians, like Bishop von Ketteler, and the historian Georg Gottfried Gervinus, who was disgusted alike by Bismarck's devious politics and by the chauvinism and gallophobia that swept Germany in the late '60s, and the philosopher Friedrich Nietzsche, who, in *Thoughts Out of Season* (1873), warned against the new preoccupation with power that seemed to be affecting government and people alike. But at least one self-styled "dyed-in-the-wool Prussian"[3] shared these fears and justified them by attributing them to the progress of *Borussismus,* of which he was the most perceptive observer from 1871 until the end of the '90s. This was the novelist—Germany's greatest of the nineteenth-century, one must add, the first to break with literary convention and, like Thackeray, Trollope and Flaubert, write about the problems of contemporary society—Theodor Fontane.

I

Fontane's Prussian credentials were unimpeachable. He was a descendant on both sides of his family of those French Huguenots who were permitted by the liberality of the Great Elector to settle in Berlin after the revocation of the Edict of Nantes — an event celebrated by Fontane in 1885 with the lines

Ein hochgemuter Fürst,
so frei wie fromm,
empfing uns hier;

2. Kenneth Attwood, *Fontane und das Preussentum* (Berlin, 1970), pp. 285 f.
3. Hans-Heinrich Reuter, *Fontane,* 2 vols. (Munich, 1968), I, 192.

und wie der Fürst des Landes
empfing uns auch sein Volk;
kein Neid war wach, nicht
Eifersucht; man öffnete das Tor uns
und hiess als Glaubensbrüder
uns willkommen.[4]

A high-spirited Prince,
As free as he was pious,
Received us here;
And, as the Prince of the country,
So also his people received us.
No envy was aroused, nor any
Jealousy; the doors were opened to us
And, as brothers in the faith,
We were made welcome.

He was born and educated in Neuruppin, the chief town of
the old Grafschaft Ruppin which had become part of the Mark
Brandenburg in 1524. Hans-Heinrich Reuter has written that
Prussian tradition was in a sense localized in Neuruppin. Two
hours away by carriage lay Fehrbellin, where the Great Elector
had defeated an invading Swedish army in 1675, in the first notable triumph of Prussian arms. From 1732 to 1736, Frederick
the Great had lived in Neuruppin as crown prince and had com-
manded the Regiment Kronprinz that was stationed there. Wu-
strau at the southern end of the Ruppiner See was the home
of Hans Joachim von Ziethen, Frederick's most famous cavalry
general, and Rheinsberg, twenty kilometers to the north, was
Frederick's residence from 1736 until he became king in 1740
and then became the home of his brother Prince Henry and
the center of a *fronde* against Berlin and Sans Souci.

All of these memories influenced Fontane when he became
a writer. His first published works were songs and ballads, the
most popular of which dealt with Prussian themes or with per-

4. Fontane, *Sämtliche Werke,* XX, 272.

sonalities like Georg Freiherr von Derfflinger, the victor at Fehrbellin, and Frederick's marshals Ziethen and Keith. His first notable prose work, *Wanderings through Mark Brandenburg*, was rich in historical recollection and anecdote; and his deep patriotism and his admiration of the Prussian military tradition doubtless had much to do with his decision to follow the campaigns of 1864, 1866, and 1870 as a war correspondent, in the last case at considerable risk. But then, Fontane always felt himself to be "ein Märkischer," and as the protagonist of his novel *Der Stechlin* said of service in Prussia's wars, "For a *Märkischer* the essential thing is to have been there. The rest is in God's hand."[5]

In the middle of the '50s, Fontane had written a review of Gustav Freytag's novel *Debit and Credit* and had cited a passage in which Freytag said that the collection of territorial fragments that the Hohenzollerns had welded into a state could never again be dissolved into its constituent parts. Fontane wrote: "This is not merely balm for a German and Prussian heart, but is as true as it is beautiful. . . . Prussia is the state of the future."[6] But it was precisely this faith that he lost in the years that followed the *Reichsgründung*. Indeed, Prussia became for him, not a force for the future, but more and more a state that had lost its way, its sense of identity, and its moral force, a state whose great days lay in the remote past. He expressed this view in his last and most political novel, *Der Stechlin*, which was published in 1898, through the mouth of the pastor Lorenzen:

> "We have had, if we look back, three great epochs. . . . Perhaps the greatest . . . was that under the soldier-king [Frederick William I]. He was a man who cannot be praised enough, and wonderfully fitted to his time and, at the same time, ahead of it. He not only stabilized the kingdom but also—what was much more important—created the foundations for a new time and, in the place of unsteadiness and selfish rule by many and

5. Fontane, *Sämtliche Werke*, VIII (*Der Stechlin*), 8.
6. Attwood, *Fontane*, p. 111.

arbitrariness, placed order and justice. Justice, that was his best *rocher de bronce* . . .

"And then came epoch two. After the first, it was not long in coming, and suddenly a country that was by nature and history unused to genius saw itself of a sudden electrified by it [the reign of Frederick II] . . .

"And then came the third age. Not great and yet again quite great. In it the poor suffering land, sunk halfway to total destruction, was illuminated, not by genius, but by inspiration, by a faith in the higher power of conscience, knowledge, and freedom [the rising against Napoleon in 1813] . . .

"And all that took a century of time. In those days, we were ahead of the others . . . certainly spiritually and morally. But the eagle with the motto 'I yield not to the sun' and the bundle of lightening bolts in its claws blazes no more, and the inspiration is dead."[7]

What had happened to the values that had sustained Prussia in its three great epochs? They had, in Fontane's view, been corrupted by success, and this took several forms, which fascinated and horrified him as early as 1871.

In the first place, it was clear to him that the army, which he had always admired, had changed in unpleasant ways as a result of its victories in 1866 and 1870. It was attracting people who were motivated, not by a sense of duty and service, but by meaner instincts. In the very year of unification, Fontane wrote in one of his war books of the young Prussian lieutenants and assessors who were moving into Alsace and Lorraine and (perhaps reflecting that Germany had been conquered by Prussia just as France had) spoke of the dubious blessing of being ruled by "careerists, adventurers, the restless, and the ambitious."[8] Even worse, the army was beginning to have an exalted opinion of its position in the state, which affected officers in field grade as well as those in command and staff positions.

7. Fontane, *Sämtliche Werke,* VIII, 252–53.
8. Ibid., XVI (*Aus den Tagen der Okkupation*), 485 ff.

Fontane found the emphasis upon *Schneidigkeit* (energy, smartness, dash) that characterized the new breed of officers ridiculous, writing, "A strong percentage of our war heroes, measured by the new measure of *Schneidigkeit*, would look like old aunties [*Susen*]";[9] but he took more seriously the arrogance and bad manners of the formerly modest Prussian lieutenant. He wrote to his daughter in August 1880: "A lieutenant should be only a lieutenant and, even if he is with the Ziethen hussars, must give up wanting to be a demigod or anything exceptional at all."[10] The new visibility of the army, the new garrison tone, the "ewige Drill," the assumption that a label stuck on you by the state was a guarantee of status worried Fontane; and the word *Borussismus* began to creep into his correspondence to describe a phenomenon that he always carefully distinguished from true Prussianism and once described as "the lowest form of culture that there is."

The disturbing thing about all this was that the army's pretensions were being accepted by the Prussian middle class, which had given itself over to a mindless jingoism ever since the victories of 1871. As a result, Fontane wrote in a curiously veiled passage in one of his war books, the country was endangered by an entirely new spirit of Potsdam, which had nothing to do with the soldier-king and his son, but was "an unholy amalgam . . . of absolutism, militarism and philistinism. . . . A breath of unfreedom, of artificiality, of the contrived blows through it all and oppresses any soul that has a greater need to breathe freely than to get into line."[11] When he wrote his first novel, *Before the Storm* (1874), about the rising of 1813, Fontane told his publisher that it was intended to combat the false patriotism of the last years. His book, he said, "struck a

9. Attwood, *Fontane*, p. 282.
10. Ibid., p. 279.
11. Fontane, *Sämtliche Werke*, XVI, 496.

blow for religion, morality, and the fatherland, but was full of hatred against the 'blue cornflower' and 'With God for King and Fatherland,'—that is, against the windy spouting and caricature of that trinity."[12] In the novels that followed, references to the pervasive militarism of middle-class society were numerous. In *Frau Jenny Treibel* (1892), Fontane caricatured the kind of person, all too numerous in Bismarckian and Wilhelmine Germany, who believed that an officer's commission in the army reserve made him a superior being whose opinions had more weight than those of mere civilians; and in *L'Adultera* (1882), Melanie von Straaten, reading the visiting card of a caller, says, "Lieutenant in the reserve of the Fifth Dragoon Regiment . . . Abhorrent to me, these everlasting lieutenants! There are no human beings any more!"[13]

One of the worst aspects of this progressive militarization was that it tended, in Fontane's view, to spread formalistic and artificial ethical concepts and standards that had deleterious social effects. Thus, the old military concept of honor had been translated, in civilian life, into a cruel and unnatural code of etiquette that imprisoned the upper classes in a moral straitjacket. As early as 1883, Fontane had hit out at this in his novel *Schach von Wuthenow*, which tells the story of a young officer who kills himself because he is forced by considerations of military honor to take a course of action that he fears will lead to a degree of social ridicule that he will not be able to tolerate. After the young man's death, Fontane's spokesman, a staff captain named von Bülow, says:

> I have belonged to this army long enough to know that "honor" is its every third word. A dancer is charming "on my honor"; a horse is magnificent "on my honor"; yes, I have even had moneylenders recommended to me as superb "on my honor."

12. Reuter, *Fontane*, II, 595.
13. Fontane, *Sämtliche Werke*, IV (*L'Adultera*), 41.

And this constant talking about honor, about a false honor, has confused the concept and made real honor dead.[14]

In a more extended treatment of this problem, in perhaps Fontane's greatest novel, *Effi Briest* (1895), a Prussian bureaucrat sacrifices his family happiness, with predictably tragic consequences for his wife, to this artificial code of honor, recognizing that his action is irrational, but insisting that society depends upon the inviolability of its taboos.

Beneath Fontane's concern over militarism on the one hand and the spread of a spurious morality on the other was a feeling that there was something even more fundamentally wrong with society. The classes that had in the past sustained the Prussian kingdom no longer showed the capacity to do so. The aristocracy had succumbed to a kind of totemism that convinced him that it was losing its originality, spontaneity, and moral energy; the middle class had lost its self-reliance.

Fontane's criticism of the aristocracy is worth emphasizing in view of the almost unqualified admiration and affection he showed them in the first part of his career as a writer. No one who reads *Wanderings through Mark Brandenburg* can fail to be struck by the author's praise of the virtues that marked their life on the land—simplicity, truthfulness, naturalness, and a strong feeling for duty, right, and order. He takes an obvious delight in the great originals that the landed nobility had produced over the centuries—like the Quitzows, for example, who in the first years of the fifteenth century laid waste the Mark in the name of freedom from centralized authority, until their power was broken by Frederick of Nuremberg, the first Hohenzollern *Kurfürst*; or Johann Friedrich Adolf von der Marwitz, the uncle of Stein's antagonist, who refused to carry out Frederick II's order to plunder Schloss Hubertusburg, was stripped of his command, and later had written on his gravestone "Chose disfavor when

14. Ibid., II (*Schach von Wuthenow*), 383–84.

obedience would not bring honor"; or Yorck von Wartenburg, who broke his king's alliance with Napoleon by going over to the Russians at Tauroggen in 1812.

But in the years after 1871, Fontane came to believe that the spontaneity and love of freedom that had once motivated the landed nobility had disappeared, while their other good qualities had become calcified, surviving only as items in a catalogue of specifically Prussian virtues that were constantly cited to justify special privilege. An illustration is his portrait of the wife of Chief Forester Katzler in *Der Stechlin,* a princess by birth, whose conversation consists largely of disquisitions on Prussian excellences that are beyond the reach of other peoples. "What is incumbent on us," she says to her resigned husband, "is not joy in life, or even real love, but simply duty," to which her husband answers ironically, "To be sure, Ermyntrud. We are agreed on that. Moreover, that is something specifically Prussian. We are distinguished by it from other countries. . . . But there are differences. Degrees."[15]

When he touched on this aristocratic form of *Borussismus* — this tendency to regard Prussianism as a superior form of culture — Fontane was content in his novels to confine himself to the use of caricature. In his letters, however, particularly in those to confidants like Georg Friedländer, he made no bones about his growing contempt for a class that, on the one hand, lived in the inflexible conviction that the country could not survive without them, and, on the other, accepted the tariffs and subventions that a complacent government granted them and opposed every tendency that could be considered progressive or even modern. In 1892, in words that recall Stein's great attack on the landed aristocracy, he wrote, "Now I see all too clearly what's wrong with our first estate: the percentage of ill educated among them is too great." A year later, he wrote: "That

15. Ibid., VIII, 164.

we now, in my view, make such a terribly retarded impression [is due to the fact] that thousands of these personalities from the stone age are running around."[16] Even more unequivocal was a letter written in his last year of life.

> Prussia, and to some extent all Germany, is sick because of its East Elbians. Our aristocracy must be passed over; one can visit them as one visits the Egyptian Museum and bows before Ramses and Amenophis, but to rule the country for their sake in the delusion that this nobility is the country, that is our misfortune, and, as long as this situation continues, a further development of German power and reputation is unthinkable.[17]

There was a time when Fontane had believed that the middle class was destined to replace the aristocracy as the leading estate in the realm, sustained by those *Bürger* virtues that he described as "property, respect for law, and the feeling of freedom that flows from the first two." Even in his last years he could write:

> I am always happy when I read names like Lisco, Lucä, Gropius, Persius, Hensel, Thaer, Körte, Dieterici, Virchow, Siemens, because I am reminded that in these flourishing families, now in the second and third generation, a new aristocracy is forming, even if without the "von," from which the world really gets something, contemporary models that advance it morally and intellectually (for to provide models is the real task of an aristocracy), and which doesn't seek its mission in life in the egotistical pickling of dead things.[18]

But he was all too conscious of the fact that these represented a tiny minority of the middle class, and that, for the rest, the old *Bürgersinn* (Bürger ethos) had not survived the liberal defeat of the '60s and the easy affluence of the first years of unifica-

16. Attwood, *Fontane*, p. 201.

17. Theodor Fontane, *Briefe in zwei Bänden*, ed. Gotthard Erler (Berlin, 1968), II, 419.

18. Attwood, *Fontane*, p. 221.

tion. The new *Besitzbürgertum* was characterized by materialism, political conformity, and a desperate desire to effect a
symbiotic relationship with the aristocracy; and Fontane's opinion of them was summed up in the remark of a character in
Der Stechlin, who says of a mill owner, "Gundermann is a bourgeois and a parvenu, therefore just about the worst thing anyone can be."[19]

II

How was one to revitalize a society that showed serious signs
of being moribund? Fontane was too conservative to desire a
thoroughgoing social revolution, and so—like a good Prussian
—he entertained the possibility that, as had happened not in-
frequently in the history of Brandenburg-Prussia, the energies
of the country might be galvanized by the force of personality,
by the coming of a gifted and determined ruler who could in-
spire his subjects to better things. Such a ruler came to the throne
in 1888, in the person of William II, and initially Fontane placed
as high hopes in him as Bettina von Arnim had in Frederick
William IV. He wrote in his diary:

> There was a general sigh of relief when the period of rule by
> sickness and women came to an end, and the youthful William
> II took the reins in his hand. It was high time. Everybody had
> the feeling that the horse of custom could not go on trotting
> in its usual way, avoiding the abyss by mere instinct, but that
> now a director was there who would not leave everything to
> chance.[20]

Fontane's hopes were not, of course, realized, but it is interesting to note how long his sympathies remained with the new
ruler and how shrewdly he analyzed William's fundamental

---

19. Fontane, *Sämtliche Werke,* VIII, 162.
20. Attwood, *Fontane,* p. 190.

problem. In a remarkable letter to his friend Friedländer in April 1897, he wrote:

> What pleases me about the Kaiser is the total break with the old, and what doesn't please me about the Kaiser is the desire, in contrast to this, to restore the very old. In a certain sense, he frees us from the empty forms and appearances of the old Prussianism, . . . he orders new trousers for himself, in every sense, instead of having the old ones patched. He is completely unpetty, he is energetic, he understands completely that a German emperor is something different from a margrave of Brandenburg. He has a million soldiers and also wants a hundred battleships; he dreams (and I give him credit for this) of a humiliation of England. Germany shall be uppermost in everything and anything. All of that—and whether it is intelligent and realizable I leave aside—affects me sympathetically, and I would willingly follow him on his high-wire performance if I saw that he had the right kind of chalk under his feet and the right kind of balancing rod in his hands. But he hasn't. He wants to attain, if not the impossible, at least the extremely dangerous, with false weapons and inadequate means; he believes that he can provide for the new with the completely old; he wants to establish the modern with weapons found in the old clothes attic.

The resources that the new ruler needed, Fontane added, were money, intelligence, and inspiration; and, if he could be sure of them, he would find that his fifty million Germans were united behind him and ready to face any trial. But, he added, "he will not attain that with grenadier helmets, medals, streamers on banners, and the poor provincial nobility 'that follows its margrave through thick and thin.'"[21]

These remarks were shrewd and touched directly upon a problem that has been relatively overlooked in the literature on William II. Books upon that deplorably energetic and ultimately unfortunate monarch have never been in short supply, even in

21. Fontane, *Briefe,* II, 418.

these days when professional historians have become fascinated by *Sozialgeschichte* (social history) and in which there is a popular textbook in Western Germany—Hans-Ulrich Wehler's *Das deutsche Kaiserreich, 1871–1918*—that hardly mentions the emperor at all. But elsewhere interest in William II remains unaffected by scholarly trendiness. While the standard biography is still Michael Balfour's *The Kaiser and His Times* (1964), there has been no dearth of new books. There were two popular biographies in 1978, as well as a perceptive Swedish study, and 1982 saw a collection of essays, edited by John C. G. Röhl and Nicolaus Sombart, called *Kaiser Wilhelm II: New Interpretations.* But none of these works has much to say about the problem that Fontane alluded to—namely, William's relationship to modernity and history and, rising out of that, his conception of his role as a Hohenzollern prince who was at one and the same time king of Prussia and German emperor.

The latter question was not, of course, a new one. We have seen how it affected William's grandfather, who had stubbornly resisted the imperial title and, when he was overborne by Bismarck, had accepted it with ill grace and made as few concessions to it as possible. William I had confined his social world and his travels to the courts of Berlin, Petersburg, Schwerin, and Vienna, preferring to stay in Berlin and watch the daily march-past of his guards at the Neue Wache from the window of his palace on Unter den Linden as if life had not changed since his father's day. The ambiguity of the double position was also much on the mind of his son, later Frederick III, who—as Bismarck noted in 1870—was "dying to be emperor," and who would doubtless, if he had lived longer, have emphasized the imperial at the expense of the royal title and, under the influence of his wife's ideas, moved in the direction of a constitutional monarchy on the British model.

It was not clear at the outset which way the young William II would go. He revered his grandfather; he was proud of his

Prussian heritage; and the strongest influence on his youth had been his commission in the First Foot Guards. He later wrote that what was "highest and most holy" to him were "Prussia, the army, and all the fulfilling duties that I first encountered in this officer corps."[22] Moreover, in the first decade of his reign, he was strongly encouraged to become, in a true sense, a Prussian ruler by the man who was his closest friend and most influential advisor, Count Philipp zu Eulenburg. Eulenburg, whose love for the young emperor was equaled only by his naive belief in his sovereign's boundless intelligence, is generally credited with having persuaded William that he must rule alone, without the restraint of chancellor or Reichstag, and do so by means of the powers inherent in the Prussian kingship. As he once admitted, Eulenburg believed that "the establishment of the German empire, that is, the blending of liberal and south German . . . with Prussian blood . . . has ruined the old Prussian kingdom. A king who rules by himself, despite the fact that that is his perfect right, is unthinkable in the eyes of 'educated, progressive' people,"[23] who, in his view, were in too rich supply in non-Prussian Germany. The time had come to reassert Prussian supremacy, which he believed had been on the wane ever since 1871. A vigorous king who charted a course that was proagrarian, antiindustrial, and antiimperialist would be able to restore the prestige and power of the social condominium that had made Prussia great.

William appeared to take this advice seriously, although it apparently appealed more to his histrionic sense than to his deeper convictions. In any event, he was willing to strike the Prussian pose, and before long provincial assemblies were forced to listen

22. On the military experience upon his life and thinking, see Gordon A. Craig, *Germany, 1866–1945* (Oxford, 1978), pp. 227–30.

23. Elizabeth Hull, "Kaiser Wilhelm II and the 'Liebenberg Circle'," in *Kaiser Wilhelm II: New Interpretations,* ed. John C. G. Röhl and Nicolaus Sombart (Cambridge, 1982), p. 208.

to their ruler, displaying all the *Schneidigkeit* of the typical Potsdam lieutenant, calling down upon their labors the blessings of "our old ally of Rossbach and Dennewitz" while members of the royal suite grumbled about having to wear Frederician uniforms and learn antique ceremonials for court balls.

But this was hardly the Prussianism that Eulenburg had in mind, a return to older values and a relatively modest foreign policy. Despite his playacting, William was a modern man, much more so than his advisor. He liked speed and novelty, fast cars and telephones; he enjoyed talking to industrialists and engineers; he had pronounced views on education and modern art, which would have been beyond the comprehension of his father and his grandfather. He kept abreast of things and always knew what was *le dernier cri*. He had no desire to be cooped up in the value system and the narrow horizons of the old Prussia. Fontane was correct in his perception that William understood completely that "a German emperor was something different from a margrave of Brandenburg." From the beginning, he was fascinated by the imperial title and the possibilities inherent in it, his thoughts ranging far beyond Bismarck's view of the emperor as merely the president of a federation of German princes, whose policies were determined by a strong-willed chancellor. William was a believer in personal rule, not only because of Eulenburg's advice, but because he was convinced that, as Kaiser, he had been entrusted by God with a mission. In a letter to his mother after the appearance of Bismarck's memoirs, he wrote:

> The Crown sends its rays "by the grace of God" into palaces and hovels, and, forgive me if I say it, Europe and the world listen to hear "what is the German Kaiser saying and thinking?" and not, what is the chancellor's will! And I have recognized that Papa's idea of the continuation of the old Reich into the new was in this sense true; he always said that, and I do the same! Now and forever there is only one true emperor in

the world, and that is the German Kaiser, not in relation to his person and character, but solely by virtue of the right of a thousand-year tradition, and his chancellor must obey![24]

In the course of his reign, and particularly after 1897, when the appointments of Bernhard von Bülow and Grand Admiral Alfred von Tirpitz completed his system of personal government, William II went far toward realizing the potentialities of the imperial office as he conceived of it. Those who believe that structures are more important in history than personalities would do well to study the impress that William II put upon every aspect of domestic and foreign policy and particularly the importance of his personal decisions in the fields of naval policy, imperial expansion, war planning (his tacit acceptance of the Schlieffen plan, for instance) and alliance policy (the fateful "Nibelungen loyalty" toward Austria.) There is no question that he became the motor of German policy, and Maximilian Harden was correct when he wrote in 1902: "All the important decisions of the past twelve years have been made by him. Changes in trade policy, the buildup of the fleet, the belief in the German Reich achieving *Weltmacht* on an enormous scale, . . . relations . . . with England, the military campaign in China, all that and a lot more besides are his work."[25]

Since, however, William's confidence in his political abilities was not balanced by the kind of education that would have justified it, and since his approach to issues was generally egotistical, with little concern for substance, and always colored by his strong instinct for self-dramatization, this work was conducted in a style that contained all of the offensive elements that Bishop von Ketteler and Fontane associated with *Borussismus.* In February 1892 he told the Brandenburg provincial

24. Elizabeth Fehrenbach, *Wandlungen des deutschen Kaisergedankens, 1871–1918* (Munich, 1969), pp. 89f.

25. Maximilian Harden, "Die Feinde des Kaisers," *Die Zukunft,* XL (1902), 340.

Landtag: "Brandenburgers, we are still destined for great things, and I lead you toward glorious days!" — and from that day on, William II spoke incessantly and bombastically, in private and in public, of the great tasks that had to be accomplished beyond the boundaries of old Europe; of a German future "less in Europe than in the entire world"; and of the mission of the Hohenzollern dynasty. He talked of the superiority of German virtues, German industry, German courage, German wine, German song. He gave unwanted advice to other governments; he claimed credit for their successes; he did not hesitate to threaten them with dire consequences when their policies displeased him. This conduct decisively worsened Germany's image in the eyes of foreigners, who tended to take William at his own valuation and to regard even his most impulsive statements as reflections of Germany's policy and intentions, and led to a growing conviction that Germany was ambitious, unpredictable, and dangerous.

This worried some Germans. In her marvellously informative diary, the Baroness Spitzemberg wrote in 1902 of a conversation with Ambassador Marschall von Bieberstein, in which they had agreed that the emperor's popularity was waning, because "H. M. is too little the king of Prussia and too much the German emperor, of the dignity of which he has cobbled together a completely false conception, false in law, and false because it does not exist in the feelings of his Germans. In this way he violates ever and again the feelings of his fellow princes and the other German families, not least of all the particularistic feelings of his Prussians, particularly in those classes that are his firmest supports, the landed nobility and the conservative bureaucrats. The playing about with mystic-medieval concepts, which are dead or dying, makes him laughable."[26]

Baroness Spitzemberg had been a close friend of Prince Bis-

26. Baronin Spitzemberg, *Tagebuch,* ed. Rudolf Vierhaus (4th ed., Göttingen, 1960), p. 422.

marck and could not be expected to be objective, and her views, in any case, did not range far beyond the confines of court society. The fact was that the things that she found objectionable, and that alarmed the world outside, were not unpopular at home, and William had not falsely estimated "the feelings of his Germans." Indeed, Elizabeth Fehrenbach has shown how Germans of all classes were excited and inspired by their flamboyant ruler: "The Kaiser made possible the escape from the labyrinths of mass society; he concentrated the people's gaze on the great man, the gifted individual, the embodiment of the historical mission."[27] She cites an impressive number of Prussian *Honoratioren* from the world of affairs, the church, and the university who eulogized him for personifying the imperial idea, like the theologian Adolf Harnack in 1907: "In the heart of every German there also lives a clear image of the Kaiser which is the expression and the product of our whole history. We desire to see our Kaiser in the combination of these two images, and we thank him for revivifying the old image of the Kaiser inside us and for enriching it with new qualities."[28] Or the historian Friedrich Meinecke in 1913:

> We are not contented with the concept of our nation as a great general spiritual energy; we crave instead a leader for that nation, a leader for whom we can march through flames. . . . [The Kaiser has] united the intense concerns of the present, the strong sense that modern people have of what is necessary in the here and now, with a glowing reverence for the nation's past. . . . People who consider only the individual characteristics of his being tend to see a contradiction between his desire to assert himself in regard to contemporary events and preoccupations and his historical romanticism. But in reality his historical ideals and symbols are the spiritual means by which he inspires the

27. Elizabeth Fehrenbach, "Images of Kaiserdom," in Röhl and Sombart, p. 276.
28. Ibid.

energies of his people and keeps under effective constraint the intense pressures of modern life.[29]

Moreover, it cannot be said that William II was "too little the king of Prussia." If we leave aside the Potsdam style that was unmistakably stamped even upon his imperial image, the fact was that he ruled Germany through Prussia and used as his instrument the very East Elbian landowners whom Theodor Fontane regarded as Prussia's sickness. Fontane had predicted the disastrous results. He will not attain his objectives, he had written, with "the poor provincial nobility 'that follows its margrave through thick and thin.' . . . Where our Kaiser sees pillars [of the state] are merely feet of clay."[30] It was to the East Elbians that William sacrificed Caprivi in 1894; it was their support that he bought, by means of protective tariffs against foreign grain that could not but alienate Russia permanently, in order to get his supplemental naval bill passed in 1900 (thus alienating the British too); and it was to them that he deferred during the war, refusing, even when the shadow of possible defeat became very dark, to use his influence to force a reform of the Prussian franchise as a means of inspiring the embattled German people to new efforts by the hope of a democratic future. In May 1918, after the agrarian conservatives in the Prussian Landtag had defeated electoral reform once again, Bernhard von der Marwitz, who was to die at the front a few weeks later, wrote, "Where are the descendants of Stein and Hardenberg? I believe that even my great-grandfather would be more far-sighted than these people."[31]

As the war that his own navalism and *Weltpolitik* had brought

29. Ibid., p. 279.
30. Fontane, *Briefe*, II, 419.
31. Gerd Heinrich, *Geschichte Preussens: Staat und Dynastie* (Frankfurt am Main, 1981), p. 454.

upon his country began to go badly, as defeat became inevitable and revolution began to break out in the cities, William cast his imperial dreams behind him and reverted to the native *Borussismus* of his first years. He dreamed of setting forth, at the head of his army, like Frederick of Nuremberg against the Quitzows, to smash the insurrectionaries in his capital, or, as he put it, to write an answer to "the couple of hundred Jews and the thousand workers . . . on the pavement with machine guns."[32] He decided that, if the victorious allies insisted upon his abdication, he would abdicate as emperor but retain his Prussian title. But his own soldiers vetoed the former proposal, and the latter was lost in the rush of events. On 10 November 1918, the last Hohenzollern ruler of Prussia crossed the Dutch border into an exile that lasted for the rest of his life.

III

When one remembers that William II retained the loyalty and affection of the great majority of middle and upper class society at least until the outbreak of the war and probably for some time afterward, one cannot help thinking of Gneisenau's bitter remark in 1812, "We dare not hide from ourselves that the nation is as bad as its government."[33] This remark may have been in Theodor Fontane's mind in February 1896, when—his own faith in William II badly eroded—he wrote to James Morris:

> Everything that is interesting is to be found in the fourth estate. The bourgeoisie is frightful, and the aristocracy and clerics are old-fashioned, always the same old stuff. The new, the better world begins with the fourth estate. . . . What the workers think, speak, and write has in fact overtaken the thinking, speaking, and writing of the ruling classes; it is all more genuine, more truthful, more full of life. The workers have attacked ev-

32. Ibid., p. 456.
33. Ritter, *Stein*, p. 383.

erything in a new way; they have not only new goals, but new methods of attaining them.[34]

Thirteen years after those words were written, the old Prussian ruling class was completely discredited and its leader in exile, and Prussia's future was in the hands of the working class and the parties that represented them. How Prussia fared under this new dispensation will be the subject of my last lecture.

34. Fontane, *Briefe,* II, 395f.

CHAPTER 4

Prussianism and Democracy: Otto Braun and Konrad Adenauer

When one remembers the attitude of the founding fathers of German socialism toward Prussia—that August Bebel believed that it was "the deadly enemy of all democracy" and that Wilhelm Liebknecht regarded its abolition as a task of first priority —it may seem surprising that Prussia not only survived the revolution of 1918 but did so largely as a result of decisions made by the Social Democratic party. Friedrich Ebert, in particular, the leader of the Majority Socialists in 1918, felt that the prevailing confusion in the country made it unwise for a provisional government that was having difficulty in asserting its authority over the nation to assume the task of running Prussia's internal affairs as well. When the national assembly at Weimar began its work, it agreed with him that the uncertain situation on Germany's frontiers forbade tampering with the traditional administrative structure of the country.

Prussia, then, continued as a separate entity. It had, to be sure, lost the dominating position that it had had in the Reich before 1914. Its ruling dynasty was gone; its army had been transformed into a *Reichswehr* under the authority of the national government; the new constitution deprived it of the ability to block legislation in the Reichsrat and Reichstag that threatened its own interests; and it lost its financial independence. But it remained the largest of the German states, with three-fifths of the national population, and the only one that extended from Germany's westernmost boundary to its farthest eastern and northern limits. More important, it was, for the whole history of the Weimar Republic, its most democratic state, with the socialists and their centrist and democratic allies controlling its government and a Social Democratic minister president.

These circumstances dominated its history in the republican period. Its territorial extent made it the most vulnerable of the German states to the ambitions of external powers, so that in the end it lost Memel to Lithuania; Danzig, Posen, West Prussia, and parts of Pomerania and East Prussia to the Poles; the Hutschiner Ländchen to Czechoslovakia; North Schleswig to Denmark; Eupen and Malmédy to Belgium; and the Saar (until 1935) to France; and, as we shall see, came close to losing its Rhine provinces as well. The fact that it was more democratic than the rest of the country, which was first suggested by the election results of June 1920 and became obvious after about 1926, exposed it to attack and eventual destruction by authoritarian and antidemocratic forces.

It is not my intention here to give a comprehensive and circumstantial account of these developments but rather to treat them episodically and through the thoughts and actions of two Prussian politicians, Otto Braun, minister president almost continuously from 1920 until 1933, and Konrad Adenauer, *Oberbürgermeister* of Cologne from 1917 until 1933 and president of the Prussian state council (*Staatsrat*) from 1921 to 1933.

This is a pairing of personalities that is not dissimilar to that of Stein and Marwitz in my first lecture. Adenauer, whose Prussian credentials were respectable, since his father had distinguished himself as an infantry lieutenant at Königgrätz in 1866, nevertheless had the strongest reservations toward Prussian tradition. Like Stein, whose city ordinance had made his political career possible, he was rooted in the older culture of the Roman West, and as a Roman Catholic he had little understanding of, or sympathy toward, Pomerania and the Mark. After the Second World

War, he was to say, "In the lands of the German West, there is a natural longing to escape from the confines of national narrowness into the fullness of the European consciousness."[1] Braun, proletarian in origin, pacifist and antimonarchist, printer and publicist for the Social Democratic party, and organizer of the rural workers against the large landholders, was nevertheless Prussian to the core, with a deep and abiding affection for his native East Prussia. Both men were convinced democrats and dedicated to the survival of the German republic, but, while Braun was sure that this goal would be possible only if Prussia's integrity were maintained so that it might serve as an *Ordnungszelle*, a guarantee of order and democracy in the country, Adenauer believed that Germany's democratic future depended upon a reconciliation with the old enemy France, even at the expense of Prussian integrity. These were more than tactical differences, for although it is true that Adenauer's policy like Bismarck's was often experimental and inductive, determined less by firmly conceived goals than by prevailing circumstances and resources, his dream of a Franco-German rapprochement survived the tragic history of the Weimar Republic and the Nazi regime that followed it and was to animate his policy as federal chancellor after 1949. In the years after 1919, its more tentative formulation was bound to lead to conflict with the stubborn East Prussian socialist.

I

That Braun and Adenauer were to travel different tracks was clear as early as the winter of 1918–19, when Germany was in the grip of military defeat and domestic revolution and the future was obscure. On 23 January 1919, the first Prussian government of the republican era met to debate a proposal that had

1. Golo Mann, "Konrad Adenauer: Staatsmann der Sorge," *Frankfurter Allgemeine Zeitung,* 14 February 1976.

been drafted by Hugo Preuss of the Reich ministry of the interior for submission to the national assembly, which was beginning its work on a new German constitution. In his draft, Preuss declared that the separate existence of Prussia had, in the new political circumstances, "lost all meaning," that Prussia had "no inherent right to continued existence, since it was an unnatural construct, the result of successfully ended wars and dynastic legacies."[2] In this view, Prussia had outlived its usefulness, and its dissolution was necessary for political as well as economic reasons.

Preuss's view was shared by a fair proportion of liberal opinion —the historian Friedrich Meinecke was one of his strongest supporters—and by the Communists, the radical left wing of the socialist movement, and even by a not inconsiderable number of Majorityites. But it found little sympathy in the Prussian state ministry on 23 January. For the most part, the objections were colored by the uncertainty concerning the nature of the peace terms, which the allies had not yet released, and Minister President Hirsch argued, for instance, that a dissolution or partition of Prussia would simply play into the hands of the Entente. But one participant in the discussion took a wider view and related the issue to Germany's political future. The minister of agriculture, Otto Braun, said that he could sympathize with Preuss's desire for a unitary, democratic German republic. But, even so, in order to attain it "one should not cut up the great states that must form the heart of the new republic . . . one should not destroy the new, the democratic Prussia." Instead of embarking upon a course that, under the guise of unity, would atomize Germany into a large number of small states, it would be better to think of effective linkages between the Prussian and Reich governments that would eliminate admin-

2. Susanne Miller and Heinrich Potthoff, eds., *Die Regierung der Volksbeauftragten, 1918–19* (Düsseldorf, 1966), Document No. 105, p. 249.

istrative duplication, provide effective coordination of policy, and serve the cause of order and democracy.[3]

Braun's remarks were made at a time when the threat of atomization was very real, not least of all because of the pressures of external powers along the eastern frontiers and in the lands bordering the Rhine. With respect to the latter, the French government had made it abundantly clear during the peace negotiations in Paris that, for security reasons, it desired the greatest possible control over the left bank of the Rhine, and this knowledge had had two results in the Rhineland. An active separatist movement had appeared, under the leadership of a Wiesbaden lawyer named Dorten, and was being encouraged by the French, and, ostensibly to combat this, a loose grouping of local politicians from the larger towns had begun to hold meetings to discuss means of forestalling the loss of the area to France. As early as 9 November 1918, the day on which the revolution broke out in Berlin, the Center party organization in Cologne, after discussions with the editors of the *Kölnische Zeitung* and an activist priest named Dr. Josef Froberger, sent a delegation to the city's *Oberbürgermeister* Konrad Adenauer to win his support for the creation of an autonomous state in the Rhineland. Adenauer was apparently interested but noncommittal, and he temporized; but the discussions continued, and on 1 February 1919 Adenauer presided over a meeting of representative Rhenish politicians in the Cologne Rathaus. Before this body, in a speech that lasted for more than three hours, he discussed the history of Franco-German relations and gave a not unsympathetic view of France's concern for its own security. Then he said:

> In the opinion of our enemies, Prussia is the evil spirit of Europe;
> . . . Prussia is the land that caused the war. . . . In their view,
> Prussia was ruled by a war-hungry, unprincipled, militaristic

---

3. Hagen Schulze, *Otto Braun oder Preussens demokratische Sendung* (Frankfurt am Main, 1977), p. 254.

caste and by the Junkers, and Prussia ruled Germany, even those people of Western Germany who in general outlook and temperament are sympathetic with the Entente peoples. If Prussia were divided and the western parts of Germany combined as a federal state, a West German republic, then the domination of Germany by a Prussia ruled by the spirit of the east and by militarism would be made impossible, and the influence of those circles who until the revolution dominated Prussia, and therefore Germany, would be definitely liquidated, even if they recovered from the revolution. This West German republic would, because of its size and economic importance, play a significant role in the new German Reich and would consequently be able to influence the foreign policy of Germany in its peaceful spirit.

Such a solution would be acceptable to England, since it would form the most secure basis for European peace. . . . It would demonstrate to France that the rightfully feared Prussia would no longer exist after the creation of the West German republic, that the restoration of the feared Hohenzollern dynasty was prevented for all time by such partition, and that . . . the antimilitaristic and peace-loving tendencies in Germany had won the upper hand.[4]

This speech had a pronounced effect upon its auditors, and, after some discussion, the gathering adopted with unanimity a resolution that disclaimed any sympathy for plans aimed at the detachment of the left bank or other parts of the Rhine provinces from Germany but declared that, "in view of the fact that a partition of Prussia is now being seriously considered, we charge a special committee elected by ourselves with the task of preparing plans for the establishment of a West German republic within the constitutional framework of the German Reich and based on the Reich constitution to be drafted by the German national assembly."[5]

In Adenauer's authorized biography, the argument is advanced

4. Karl Dietrich Erdmann, *Adenauer in der Rheinlandpolitik nach dem ersten Weltkrieg* (Stuttgart, 1966), pp. 221 f.

5. Ibid., p. 229.

that all of this was nothing but a ruse to enable the Cologne *Oberbürgermeister* "to lay his hands on the separatist movement which was growing to dangerous underground dimensions, to get control of it and, once control was gained, to strangle it."[6] As proof, the point is made that he never called any meetings of the special committee mentioned in the resolution of 1 February. It seems more likely that the reason why the committee died a-borning was that, in view of the strong position taken by the Prussian state ministry and — as a result of that and Friedrich Ebert's position — the failure of the Preuss proposal in the national assembly, no strong popular support developed, even in the Rhineland, for the idea of a West German republic separated from Prussia. This did not mean that Adenauer's arguments on 1 February had not been seriously meant or that he had abandoned them for want of public interest. Indeed, four and a half years later, he was to revive his West German plan with greater determination.

The occasion this time was the near financial collapse of both the Reich and the Prussian government as a result of the policy of passive resistance that had been adopted by the Cuno government in the months following the French occupation of the Ruhr. That policy had been a fiasco, which had succeeded only in hardening the French determination to gain territorial guarantees (productive pledges) in the Rhineland against further reparations defaults, while at the same time exceeding the resources of the German government and debauching its currency. When the Stresemann government came to power in August 1923 and ended passive resistance a month later, the situation had become so critical that it seemed quite possible that the national government, if it wished to stabilize the currency, might

6. Paul Weymar, *Adenauer: His Authorized Biography*, trans. from the German (New York, 1957), p. 48.

be forced to stop all financial support for the Rhenish provinces before the end of the year.

This prospect had an exciting effect on the mayors of the Rhenish and Westphalian cities and on other western politicians who were confronted with a renewal of separatist agitations, which were particularly strong in Aachen, Trier, Koblenz, and Bonn. A group of them requested a meeting with the Reich government at Hagen on 25 October and in preparation held private discussions at Barmen in the occupied zone on the twenty-fourth. At Barmen, responding to proposals for offensive action against what was assumed to be an attempt by France to promote annexation by local subversion, Adenauer returned to his suggestions of February 1919. Unless the Reich could promise support of a tangible nature, the best way of checking, and at the same time reassuring, the French would be the creation of a West German republic, preferably as a part of the German Reich but — since mere separation from Prussia would probably no longer satisfy France — if necessary separated from it. In either case, Germany would derive advantage, for as a price for the establishment of a West German republic it could insist on an end of allied occupation of the Rhineland. Moreover, if that republic were separated from the Reich, significant alleviation of the Versailles Treaty would be necessary.

Adenauer carried these arguments to Hagen, where he and other western politicians met with the Reich chancellor, Gustav Stresemann, and other cabinet ministers and with the head of the Prussian government since 1920, Otto Braun. Adenauer's authorized biography is again misleading, intimating that Stresemann and Braun were both quite ready to abandon the Rhine provinces to their own resources, even if this meant increasing dependence upon, and eventual absorption by, France. The reality seems to be that Stresemann urged that no precipitate action be taken, promising that the Reich would support the Rhine provinces as long as possible and that, meanwhile, he would seek international backing and pressure upon the French from London and Washington. He expressed extreme skepticism with respect to Adenauer's plan, intimating that it might facilitate the achievement of French ambitions, but he did not oppose the establishment of a commission to open political talks with the French, as Adenauer had proposed.

This proposal Otto Braun felt was a mistake. He was prepared, he said, to face up to the fact that the financial difficulties of Prussia and the Reich had given France the opportunity to gain what it had been seeking ever since 1919, but he was not willing to collaborate in the achievement of that result. No political talks should be held with the French. To show that degree of weakness could only encourage other separatists and subversive movements, in places like Saxony and Thuringia and Bavaria. Braun was overruled at Hagen, but he restated his position at a meeting of the Reich cabinet and the *Länder* on 13 November:

> France has been victorious with its tactics; its goal is political and economic domination of the occupied area. . . . What is to happen to help the Rhineland? In my view, we are no longer in a position to help. We must, so to speak, leave the occupied zone to its fate. [But] it is impossible to give such far-reaching powers to a commission as the Reich government intends. That would be tantamount to establishing a [new] government [in the Rhineland]. From now on, everything that happens in the occupied zone must appear to have been extorted.[7]

The Prussian government might, Braun was saying, be forced to admit its powerlessness to affect the course of events, but in no circumstances would it agree to a separation of the occupied zone from Prussia, and the Reich government shouldn't do so either by encouraging a commission to enter into talks

7. Schulze, *Otto Braun,* p. 442.

with the French. Nor was Braun content to believe that the financial situation was necessarily as hopeless as it had appeared in October, and when reports of the Prussian ministries of finance and the interior at the beginning of December revealed expedients that could be used to help the unemployed in the occupied zone, he was encouraged to take a stronger stand against both the Reich government and the western politicians. In a speech on 5 December 1923 before the Prussian Landtag, he attacked the Rhenish commission that had been authorized at Hagen and had since then been talking with French officials about possible changes in the status of the occupied territory:

> To all these efforts the Prussian government has shown determined opposition. And it will fight them in the future with all the means at its disposal. That goes also for all plans to lay claim to rights of sovereignty in different areas of public life for ad hoc committees or bodies formed by them in violation of legal and constitutional provisions. . . . The government of the [Prussian] state must refuse to assent, expressly or tacitly, to any legal alterations, whatever form they may take. And even more it rejects emphatically any territorial change of Prussian territory and any action prejudicing Prussian rights of sovereignty.[8]

This speech, and Braun's added promise to alleviate the financial and economic problems of the Rhenish provinces, effected a sensible change of mood in that area, as the Prussian minister of the interior reported a few days later. Popular interest in the establishment of a West German republic now seeped rapidly away. Adenauer doggedly pursued his plans in contacts with the French president of the Rhineland Commission, Tirard, and, through the German industrialist Hugo Stinnes, with other French agencies, but his efforts were brusquely repudiated in 1924 by Gustav Stresemann, now Reich foreign minister, who remarked tartly on Adenauer's undue sensitivity to French secu-

8. Ibid., p. 444.

rity needs. The Rhineland question now went back to the diplomats and was regulated at the London Conference and by the Dawes Plan; but there is little doubt that Otto Braun helped influence that result by his strong speech of 5 December 1923.

II

Although the Rhenish question exacerbated relations between Braun and Adenauer, these were already in bad repair as a result of their official relationship. Since May 1921, Adenauer had been president of the Prussian state council, a body that had originally been thought of as a kind of surrogate for the former chief of state and also as a balance to the state ministry on the one hand and the Landtag on the other, but had been given no explicit powers to realize those functions, save a vague right to give opinions on proposed legislation. Immediately after his election, the Rhenish leader began a systematic campaign to increase the powers of the council at the expense of the ministry, seeking to acquire rights of collaboration and control in the legislative function. Braun saw this as an attack upon his own authority and reacted violently.

Conflict was inevitable in any case. To the casual observer Braun and Adenauer might seem antipodal natures. The East Prussian with his tall, slightly bowed frame, hooked nose, and dark heavy eyebrows, was angular in his movements, brusk and often violent in his speech, although not without a certain grim humor, and indeed resembled the Junkers of his homeland so closely that it was rumored that his real father was a large landholder (*Grossgrundbesitzer*). The Rhinelander, slender and graceful, with an impassive, almost Mongol face that concealed his thoughts, was sophisticated in his thinking, *rusé* in his methods, and given to nuances rather than outright declarations. But in essentials the two men were alike, and in their similarities destined to be adversaries. Both were what the Germans call

Herrschernaturen, intent on dominating any situation in which they found themselves, jealous of their prerogatives and intent on enhancing them, intolerant of equals, suspicious of strong personalities who might challenge their position, secretive toward their own subordinates—all traits, one is reminded, that were characteristic of Bismarck in his time.

Braun, therefore, was bound to oppose Adenauer's efforts to increase the powers of his office. He regarded the state council, in any case, as superfluous and, since it claimed to represent the provincial organs of self-government, as an encouragement to particularism, and he made it clear that he wished it to be abolished by constitutional amendment as soon as possible. Ignoring all of Adenauer's demands to be informed in advance of legislative proposals and instructions to the Prussian delegates to the federal council, he so infuriated the president of the Staatsrat that, at the end of 1922, he formally complained to the highest court in the land, accusing Braun of unconstitutional behavior. Because of the Ruhr crisis, the case was not decided until the end of 1923, when the court in effect rejected Adenauer's complaint, while counseling Braun to treat him more tactfully. This was not advice that Braun was likely to follow in the wake of Adenauer's Rhenish policy, which convinced him that the Cologne *Oberbürgermeister* was at heart a separatist and potentially an agent of France. As a result, the state council became a body without real functions, and Adenauer's role in Prussian politics became peripheral in the period that followed.

One wonders what might have happened if these two gifted, imaginative, and strong-willed personalities had been able to overcome their temperamental differences and combine their talents in the effort to save the Weimar Republic through the agency of Prussian democracy. There is no doubt that Adenauer was the most reliable ally that Braun could have found. He was the leader of that section of the Center party that believed in close cooperation with the Social Democrats, unlike Heinrich Brüning, Monsignor Kaas, and Franz von Papen. He was convinced, as Braun was, that it would be good if the Social Democrats were represented in the national government, as they had not been since 1920. In 1926, when his name was put forward as candidate for the Reich chancellorship, he made acceptance conditional upon the formation of a "great coalition" that would include the socialists, and, when this was rejected by the German Peoples party, whose chairman told him that it was "totally out of the question for them to join the socialists in a government," responded that the idea that the socialists could be "simply excluded . . . could really make one weep."[9] He would have had no fundamental disagreement with Braun's idea, when political extremism began to increase in the country after 1929, of strengthening the prospects of democracy by linkages between the Prussian and Reich governments, through combinations between ministries and agencies. Finally, Adenauer and Braun were in agreement about where the most dangerous threat to democracy lay—not in the first instance in the National Socialist party, but in those unreconciled conservative forces, particularly the military and the old landed aristocracy, which were hoping to use Hitler to destroy the republic. Whether an alliance between Braun and Adenauer could have prevented a victory of the right is of course questionable, but it is a pity that their energies were not equally joined in the fight.

III

It was a fight that Braun could not hope to win alone, because before it reached its critical point, he had lost the support of the president of the republic, the old Field Marshall Paul von Hindenburg. In the first years after Hindenburg's election in 1925, a surprising intimacy had grown between the two men.

9. See Fritz Stern, *The Failure of Illiberalism: Essays on the Political Culture of Modern Germany* (New York, 1972), p. 182.

An East Prussian himself, Hindenburg was favorably impressed by Braun's stature (he was taller by a hand than Hindenburg himself), by his forthrightness, and by his ability to think in other than party terms. His original suspicion of Braun as a pacifist was overcome when he discovered that, like himself, the Prussian minister president was an impassioned huntsman. Arnold Brecht reports the president as saying, "First he wouldn't shoot at all, and now he shoots like crazy! [*Erst wollt' er gar nicht schiessen, und nun schiesst er rein wie doll!*]."[10] Helmuth von Gerlach recalled Hindenburg's telling a friend, "Just think how often you get false information about a person! My friends in Hannover told me that Otto Braun was a fanatical inciter of trouble. And now I see that he is a completely reasonable man with whom one can talk about anything."[11] Certainly they did talk about a great number of things, for the president fell into the habit of consulting Braun on political problems that perplexed him, and more often than not he followed his advice.

This was not to last. Hindenburg was not a strong man or one who was capable of resisting the pressures of his own class and his own profession, and in the long run his fellow landowners and officers persuaded him to turn against his friend.

The agrarians' hatred of Braun went back to the first days after the revolution, when as Prussian minister of agriculture he had sought to win legal work contracts for agricultural laborers and had become embroiled with the Pomeranian Landbund who accused him of Bolshevism. This accusation followed him through the years and found its bitterest formulations at the end of the '20s, when the Reich government, under the influence of pressure groups representing big agriculture, began a program known as *Osthilfe,* tariffs and subventions to ease the economic troubles of the great East Elbian grain growers.

10. Arnold Brecht, *Lebenserinnerungen,* 2 vols. (Stuttgart, 1966–67), II, 20.
11. Schulze, *Braun,* p. 489.

This return to Bismarck's preferential policy struck Braun as being both unjust and potentially unproductive, for he believed that the economic health of East Prussia would be best served by the expropriation of unprofitable estates and a systematic policy of partition, resettlement, and industrialization. It should not be the policy of the state, he declared in the Prussian chamber in December 1928, to come to the aid of heavily mortgaged estates regardless of the culpability of their owners for this condition: "It is not in the interest of the state to see to it that these few hundred *Grossbesitzer-Existenzen* are maintained in their social position!"[12] Since the *Osthilfe* had to be administered through Prussian agencies, Braun sought to control it by making judgments of justified need, confiscating bankrupt estates, and dispensing aid to middle-range and small farmers.

In the long run, this effort did not succeed in derailing *Osthilfe*. It did, however, arouse the fury of the great landowners, and this inevitably affected Braun's relations with Hindenburg, for in October 1927 the president had himself become a *Grossgrundbesitzer,* thanks to the donation by a group of industrialists and landholders of an estate at Neudeck in East Prussia. In his visits to his new holdings, Hindenburg heard a lot about the iniquities of his friend Braun, for Neudeck was a gathering place of the cream of the East Prussian landed aristocracy, Dohnas, Eulenburgs, Mirbachs, Cramons. Eluard von Oldenburg-Januschau, a declared foe of Braun, owned the neighboring estate, and Freiherr von Gayl, director of the Ostpreussische Landgesellschaft, was a frequent visitor.

Braun's position would have been less vulnerable if he had not at the same time lost the confidence of the military. He had, in fact, been in almost continuous conflict with the Reichswehr command ever since 1919 because of its tendency, under the guise of raising auxiliary forces for border protection, to

12. Ibid., p. 678.

enter into relations with, and to arm and support, antirepublican organizations like the free corps that supported Kapp in 1920 and the *Arbeitskommandos* that were stationed at Küstrin in 1923 and were barely prevented from making a putsch against the Stresemann government. In 1923, Braun's minister of the interior, Carl Severing, negotiated an agreement with Reichswehr minister Otto Gessler that stipulated that the Prussian government must be informed of all plans for the protection of the frontiers, including location of munitions dumps, organizations to be involved, and mobilization plans. But it was soon clear that the military leaders were systematically violating this understanding. In 1926, Severing's successor, Albert Grzesinski, documented their cold-blooded attempts to build up a "Black Reichswehr" and their intimate ties with illegal organizations like the Wiking-Bund and the Sportverein Olympia. "Instead of creating a defensive troop for the security of the Reich and the [Prussian] state," Grzesinski reported, "the Reichswehr is creating a power that represents a constant threat to internal peace and order."[13] Braun immediately announced that he would stop cooperating with the Reichswehr in matters of border defence until Hans von Seeckt's successor as chief of army command, General Heye, provided him with guarantees against further abuses. A new agreement was reached at the end of 1927, but within a year it was discovered that irregular forces of *Feldjäger* (chasseurs) raised during the crisis of 1923 were, despite unequivocal assurances by Heye and Reichswehr Minister Groener that they had long been disbanded, not only still in existence but actually holding exercises in Hessen-Nassau in collaboration with local National Socialists.

Braun's attempts to control army activities, his constant complaints, and his publicizing of breaches of confidence aroused mounting animosity against him in the army, and his attacks

13. Ibid., p. 611.

upon paramilitary organizations that the Reichswehr regarded as useful auxiliaries compounded his crimes in its eyes. It was his activity in this latter regard that also exhausted his credit with Hindenburg. In September 1929, the *Vossische Zeitung* reported that units of the veterans organization Stahlhelm in the Rhineland had held maneuvers, with four thousand participants, at Langenberg south of Essen in the demilitarized zone. Since this was a breach of treaty that was bound to cause foreign complications, the Prussian ministry of the interior immediately declared the Rhenish Stahlhelm an illegal organization and placed it under *Verbot,* prohibiting it from public activity. Hindenburg, who was an honorary member of the Stahlhelm, to which many of his friends belonged, took this as a personal affront and tried to persuade the Reich government to overrule Braun's action, which it could not constitutionally do. Despite entreaties from friends and party comrades, who felt that the issue was too small to justify jeopardizing his relations with the president, Braun refused to budge, on the grounds that any concession would encourage reactionary forces in the country. It was not until July 1930, in changed political circumstances, that he finally revoked the decree, although only after insisting on explicit disclaimers from the Stahlhelm leadership.

If this was a retreat on his part, it cannot be considered one that significantly affected the course of events, which was now, in any case, running strongly against Prussian democracy. On 27 March 1930, the last Reich government that could be considered a democratic one, the "great coalition" of Hermann Mueller, fell from office. Its collapse had long been predicted, and in rightist circles there had been much discussion of the nature of the succession. At the end of 1929, General Kurt von Schleicher, head of the political bureau of the Reichswehr and the same Schleicher who was reported in 1926 to have said that the Reichswehr had "had enough of the snuffling around of the Prussian government,"[14] proposed to President Hindenburg the establishment of a cabinet that would be responsible only to him, with either Ernst Scholz of the Peoples party or Heinrich Brüning of the Center as chancellor, a cabinet that would stand above the parties and would be strong enough to put an end to Prussia's sabotage of national defence and its underground campaign against the Reichswehr. In the months that followed it was clear that both the soldiers and the agrarians were counting upon an authoritarian Reich government and Hindenburg's new animus against the Prussian minister president to bring him and his government down.

IV

How that was effected and how it contributed to the fall of the Weimar Republic have been told many times, most circumstantially in Hagen Schulze's masterful biography of Otto Braun. After the era of presidential cabinets had begun, with the establishment of the Brüning government in March 1930, Braun's hope of saving the republic by means of Prussian democracy became hopeless, although it was characteristic of him not to believe that. Indeed, after the fateful national elections of September, which made the National Socialists the second largest party in the country and made Brüning dependent upon socialist votes for his Reichstag majority, Braun suggested that the time had come for a linkage between the cabinets of Prussia and the Reich in the interest of democracy, with the Prussian minister president becoming vice-chancellor. When Brüning raised this matter with Hindenburg, the president vetoed it in the strongest language. Brüning, indeed, now became suspect because of his toleration of Braun, and the Prussian minister

14. Ibid., p. 610.

president's insistence in April 1932 that the Reich government forbid public appearances of Hitler's SA and SS in the interest of internal security and his subsequent success in persuading Brüning to consider implementing his plans of land resettlement in the east cost the chancellor the support of Schleicher and Hindenburg and led to his dismissal in May 1932. As for Braun, the agrarians and soldiers were more than ever determined that his head must fall too.

I am conscious that there is a certain circularity, a kind of Viconian *ricorso,* in these lectures, which began with the conservative forces of the old Prussia uniting to drive Stein and the reformers of 1807 from office and which now end with the same forces combining against the democrat Otto Braun. The difference between the two cases is that Marwitz and his friends were persuaded that, in attacking the reformers, they were saving the real Prussia, whereas Oldenburg-Januschau and Schleicher and their associates didn't seem to care about Prussia and, indeed, by their egoism and materialism and feckless maneuvering, brought to power the man who would destroy it perhaps forever.

Braun's fall, when it came, was a pathetic end to a life spent fighting for democracy. The so-called *Preussenschlag* of 20 July 1932, when Brüning's successor, Papen, deposed the Prussian government by emergency decree for failing to maintain the public order that his own toleration of the Nazis had subverted, seemed to take the Prussian minister president by surprise, and he put up no active resistance. He was at a later date criticized for not at least resorting to the tactics that had defeated the Kapp *Putsch* in 1920, but there was no assurance that the trade unions would have tried a general strike in time of deep depression, and Braun seems to have doubted that his own police would have supported defiance of a presidential decree. He elected instead to appeal to the supreme constitutional court against the clear unconstitutionality of Papen's action, a weak expedient with a predictable result. At the end of the year, the court handed down an ambiguous verdict which agreed in the main with Braun's contention but stated that, in time of public disorder, the president had the authority to order the takeover of local police forces, as Papen had done in Prussia. Braun and the other Prussian ministers were restored to their offices, but all effective power was left in the hands of the Reich commissioner, a position that Papen continued to hold through the short Schleicher government and into the first months of Hitler's chancellorship.

Braun sought to make the most of this shadowy existence, actually attempting, during Schleicher's tenure, to interest that devious politician in combining their forces to stop Hitler. Nothing came of this proposal, although it may have persuaded Papen that Braun was still dangerous. In any event, at the first meeting of the Hitler cabinet in February 1933, Papen declared that it was absolutely necessary to get rid of the Braun government, the more so because it was blocking the dissolution of the Prussian Landtag and thus preventing new elections that the Nazis wanted in order to confirm their power in Germany's largest state.

It is at this late point that Adenauer reenters the story. The power to order the dissolution of the Landtag lay constitutionally in the hands of a three-man collegium: the minister president (Braun), the president of the Landtag (a National Socialist named Kerrl), and the president of the Staatsrat (Adenauer). Braun saw no reason to accommodate the Nazis, and Adenauer agreed with him. The new Reich cabinet, therefore, decided on a second coup d'état against Braun, and Papen and his agrarian friends persuaded the Reich president to issue a new decree, placing all of the sovereign rights of the Prussian state ministry in the hands of the Reich commissioner. When the three-man collegium met again, therefore, Papen was in Braun's chair. When asked for his views on the dissolution of the Landtag, Adenauer declared that he could not accept the legitimacy of the reformed collegium because the president's decree was unconstitutional and left the room. Papen and Kerrl did not hesitate to declare this an abstention and promptly voted the dissolution. The way was now clear for the Nazis to take full power in Prussia, for success in the forthcoming elections was assured by the fact that Papen had turned the police forces over to the direction of Hermann Goering, who saw to it that they did not interfere with the SA's reign of terror in the days before the balloting.

On the day after his stubborn refusal to give in to Papen's pressure, Konrad Adenauer telephoned to Arnold Brecht, Braun's chief advisor on constitutional matters, and told him that he would not join in the formal protest of the Prussian ministry against the Hindenburg decree that had unseated Braun. He added, "During its whole period of office, the Braun ministry has behaved in such an unfriendly fashion toward the state council that as president of the Staatsrat I do not think it suitable to give him any particular assistance."[15]

This was a demonstration of pettiness that Adenauer might have spared himself and which is unpleasant to recall. After all, Braun's political life was finished, gone with the Prussia that he had tried to preserve, killed by men who so hated his democratic Prussia that they were willing to hand it over to Adolf Hitler. Adenauer, on the other hand, although he could not have suspected it in 1933, was to have almost twenty more years of political activity after that great destroyer's work was done, and in those two decades he was not only to assure his place in history but to prove the essential consistency of his political career. In the first volume of his memoirs, which deals with the period from 1945 to 1953, Adenauer talks of the creation of the state of North Rhine-Westphalia by the British occupying forces in 1946 and writes:

> I declared that the hitherto existing Rhine province must as far as possible be tied together with western and eastern areas

15. Ibid., p. 781.

of Germany, in order to secure the left bank of the Rhine against France's demand for its separation from Germany. . . . In the formation of a great West German state inside Germany . . . lay, in my opinion, a reliable guarantee of peace in Europe. A West German state . . . offers the best assurance against actions from Germany, even after its recovery, that could lead to war. Such a . . . state would quite naturally, because of the views of its inhabitants and its whole economic structure, be bent upon cooperation with Germany's western neighbors, Belgium, Luxemburg, France, and England. . . . I expected in particular that France could gradually be persuaded that the creation of such a state provided a greater assurance of lasting peace than permanent occupation or separation of German territories. Of course, these were considerations that stretched far into the future. But in my view the conditions in Europe and the world were such that one must make plans with one's eyes on the future.[16]

This language is strongly reminiscent of Adenauer's speeches of 1919 and 1923, except that there is no mention of Prussia. But that was no longer necessary, since, thanks to its soldiers and agrarians, Prussia had committed suicide in 1933.

16. Konrad Adenauer, *Erinnerungen, 1945–53* (Stuttgart, 1965), pp. 99, 100 f.

Bibliographies
Index

Bibliographies

Chapter 1. The Failure of Reform: Stein and Marwitz

Theodor Fontane, *Sämtliche Werke*, Nymphenburg edition, ed. Edgar Gross (24 vols., Munich, 1959–75), IX–XIII (*Wanderungen durch die Mark Brandenburg*); Theodor Heuss, *Würdigungen* (Tübingen, 1955); Georg Holmsen, *Freiherr vom Stein in Selbstzeugnissen und Bilddokumenten* (Hamburg, 1975); Walther Kayser, *Marwitz* (Hamburg, 1936); F. A. L. von der Marwitz, *Aus dem Nachlasse* (2 vols., Berlin, 1852); Friedrich Meinecke, *Brandenburg, Preussen, Deutschland: Kleine Schriften zur Geschichte und Politik* (Stuttgart, 1979); Herbert Michaelis and Ernst Schraepeler, eds., *Ursachen und Folgen vom deutschen Zusammenbruch 1918–1945*, vol. XXIII (Berlin, n. d.); Peter Paret, *Clausewitz and the State* (New York, 1976); Gerhard Ritter, *Stein: Eine politische Biographie*, 3d. ed. (Stuttgart, 1958); Freiherr vom Stein, *Briefe und amtliche Schriften*, ed., W. Hubatsch (10 vols., Stuttgart, 1957–74); Freiherr vom Stein, *Denkwürdigkeiten und Briefe*, ed. L. Lorenz (Berlin, 1919); Rudolf von Thadden, *Fragen an Preussen: Zur Geschichte eines aufgehobenen Staates* (Munich, 1981); Heinrich von Treitschke, *Deutsche Geschichte*, 5 vols. (Leipzig, 1879–1894); Barbara Vogel, "Reformpolitik in Preussen, 1807–1820," in *Preussen im Rückblick*, ed. Hans-Jürgen Puhle and Hans-Ulrich Wehler (Göttingen, 1980); G. Winter, ed., *Die Reorganisation des preussischen Staates unter Stein und Hardenberg* (Berlin, 1931).

Chapter 2. Romance and Reality: Bettina von Arnim and Bismarck

Achim von Arnim and Bettina von Arnim, *Achim und Bettina von Arnim in ihren Briefe*, 2 vols. (Frankfurt am Main, 1981); Bettina von Arnim, *Werke*, ed. Gustav Konrad, 5 vols. (Frechen/Cologne, 1959–63); Hans von Arnim, *Bettina von Arnim* (Berlin, 1963); Otto von Bismarck, *Gedanken und Erinnerungen*, new ed. (Stuttgart, 1928); Otto von Bismarck, *Die gesammelten Werke*, 15 vols. (Berlin, 1924 ff.); Clemens von Brentano, *Gedichte*, ed. Wolfgang Frühwald, Bernhard Gajek and Friedhelm Kemp (Munich, 1968); Walter Bussmann, *Wandel und Kontinuität in Politik und Geschichte*, ed. Werner Pöls (Boppard, 1973); Gisela Dischner, *Bettina von Arnim: Eine weibliche So-*

zialbiographie (Berlin, 1977); Ingeborg Drewitz, *Bettine von Arnim: Romantik, Revolution, Utopie* (Cologne, 1969); Gustav Freytag, *Briefe an Albrecht von Stosch* (Leipzig, 1913); Lothar Gall, *Bismarck, der weisse Revolutionär* (Frankfurt am Main, 1980); Adolf Glassbrenner, *Der politisierende Eckensteher,* ed. Jost Hermand (Stuttgart, 1969); Theodore S. Hamerow, *The Social Foundations of German Unification, 1858–1871,* 2 vols. (Princeton, 1972); Heinrich Heine, *Werke,* ed. Martin Greiner, 2d rev. ed. (Cologne, 1962); Arthur Helps and Elizabeth Jane Howard, *Bettina: A Portrait* (New York, n. d.); Jost Hermand, ed., *Der deutsche Vormärz: Texte und Dokumente* (Stuttgart, 1967); Horst Kohl, ed., *Die politischen Reden des Fürsten Bismarck, 1847–1897,* 14 vols. (Stuttgart, 1892–1905); Helmuth Kühn and Manfred Schlösser, "Bettina von Arnim: Ein Brief," in *Preussen, Dein Spree-Athen,* ed. Hellmut Kühn (Hamburg, 1981); Luigi Magnani, *Beethovens Konversationshefte* (Munich, 1967); Friedrich Meinecke, *Preussen und Deutschland* (Munich, 1918); Friedrich Naumann, *Demokratie und Kaisertum* (Berlin, 1900); Heinrich von Treitschke, *Deutsche Geschichte,* vol. V (Berlin, 1894); K. A. Varnhagen von Ense, *Tagebücher* (Leipzig, 1862); Werner Vordtriede, *Bettina von Arnims Armenbuch* (Frankfurt am Main, 1981).

Chapter 3. The Triumph of Borussismus: *Theodor Fontane and William II*

Kenneth Attwood, *Fontane und das Preussentum* (Berlin, 1970); Michael Balfour, *The Kaiser and His Times* (London, 1964); Maurice Baumont, *The Fall of the Kaiser* (New York, 1931); Gordon A. Craig, *Germany, 1866–1945* (Oxford, 1978); Erich Eyck, *Das persönliche Regiment Wilhelms II* (Zurich, 1948); E. Fehrenbach, *Wandlungen des deutschen Kaisergedankens, 1871–1918* (Munich, 1969); Theodor Fontane, *Fontanes Briefe in zwei Bänden,* ed. Gotthard Erler, 2 vols. (Berlin, 1968); Theodor Fontane, *Sämtliche Werke,* ed. Edgar Gross, 24 vols. (Munich, 1959–73); Maximilian Harden, "Die Feinde des Kaisers," *Die Zukunft,* XL (1902); Gerd Heinrich, *Geschichte Preussens: Staat und Dynastie* (Frankfurt am Main, 1981); Hermann Oncken, *Grossherzog Friedrich I von Baden,* 2 vols. (Stuttgart, 1927); Hans-Jürgen Puhle and Hans-Ulrich Wehler, eds. *Preussen im Rückblick* (Göttingen, 1980); Hans-Heinrich Reuter, *Fontane,* 2 vols. (Munich, 1968); John C. G. Röhl and Nicolaus Sombart, eds. *Kaiser Wilhelm II: New Interpretations* (Cambridge, 1982); Baronin Spitzemberg, *Das Tagebuch der Baronin Spitzemberg: Aufzeichnungen aus der Hofgesellschaft des Hohenzollernreiches,* ed. Rudolf Vierhaus, 4th ed. (Göttingen, 1960).

Chapter 4. Prussianism and Democracy: Otto Braun and Konrad Adenauer

Konrad Adenauer, *Erinnerungen, 1945–1953* (Stuttgart, 1965); Otto Braun, *Von Weimar zu Hitler,* 3d rev. ed. (Hamburg, 1949); Arnold Brecht, *Aus nächster Nähe: Lebenserinnerungen,* 2 vols. (Stuttgart, 1966–67); Heinrich Brüning, *Memoiren, 1918–1934* (Stuttgart, 1970); Gordon A. Craig, *Germany, 1866–1945* (Oxford, 1978); Gordon A. Craig, *The Politics of the Prussian Army, 1640–1945* (Oxford, 1955); Andreas Dorpalen, *Hindenburg and the Weimar Republic* (Princeton, 1964); Karl Dietrich Erdmann, *Adenauer in der Rheinlandpolitik nach dem ersten Weltkrieg* (Stuttgart, 1966); Gerd Heinrich, *Geschichte Preussens: Staat und Dynastie* (Frankfurt am Main, 1981); Hajo Holborn, "Prussia and the Weimar Republic," in *Moderne Preussische Geschichte, 1648–1947,* ed. Otto Büsch and Wolfgang Neugebauer, vol. 3 (Berlin, 1981); Henning Köhler, *Autonomiebewegung oder Separatismus: Die Politik der "Kölnischen Volkszeitung" 1918–1919* (Berlin, 1974); Georg Kotowski, "Preussen und die Weimarer Republik," in *Moderne Preussische Geschichte, 1648–1947,* ed. Otto Büsch and Wolfgang Neugebauer, vol. 3 (Berlin, 1981); Golo Mann, "Konrad Adenauer, Staatsmann der Sorge," *Frankfurter Allgemeine Zeitung,* 14 February 1976; Susanne Miller and Heinrich Potthoff, eds., *Die Regierung der Volksbeauftragten, 1918–1919* (Düsseldorf, 1966); Hagen Schulze, *Otto Braun oder Preussens demokratische Sendung* (Frankfurt am Main, 1977); Fritz Stern, "Adenauer and a Crisis in Weimar Democracy," *Political Science Quarterly* 73, no. 1 (March 1958); Paul Weymar, *Adenauer: His Authorized Biography,* trans. from the German (New York, 1957).

Index

COMPOSED BY METRICOMP
GRUNDY CENTER, IOWA
MANUFACTURED BY THOMSON-SHORE, INC.
DEXTER, MICHIGAN
TEXT AND DISPLAY LINES ARE SET IN BEMBO

Library of Congress Cataloging in Publication Data
Craig, Gordon Alexander, 1913–
    The end of Prussia.
    (The Curti lectures ; 1982)
    Bibliography: pp. 95–97.
    Includes index.
    1. Prussia (Germany) — History — 1789–1900. 2. Prussia
(Germany) — History — 1870–   . I. Title. II. Series.
    DD417.C7 1984   943   83-40261
          ISBN 0-299-09730-7